Can You Hear the Music?

My Journey Through Madness

Ann E. Jeffers

Mad Engineer Press, LLC

This is a work of creative nonfiction. The events and conversations are portrayed to the best of the author's memory. While all the stories in this book are true, some names and identifying details have been changed to protect the privacy of the people involved.

Copyright © 2023 by Ann E. Jeffers

All rights reserved.

No portion of this book may be reproduced in any form without written permission from the publisher or author, except as permitted by U.S. copyright law.

First Edition: 2023

ISBN 979-8-9890015-0-7 (Paperback)

ISBN 979-8-9890015-1-4 (eBook)

Library of Congress Control Number: 2023915716

Front cover design by Nuno Moreira, https://nmdesign.org/.

Published by Mad Engineer Press, LLC, https://madengineerpress.com.

To Susan—my rock, my anchor, my love—for her unwavering support,

And to my kids, who give me a reason to live each and every day.

Contents

Preface

This is the true story of my journey through madness. The timeline of events—from my diagnosis with bipolar disorder to my eventual recovery—was documented meticulously in mood charts I kept and a journal I wrote in nearly daily during that time. Although this is ultimately my story and a work of creative nonfiction, I have verified the information contained in this book with the other main characters prior to publishing to ensure it is as accurate as possible. The names and characteristics of some individuals have been changed to protect their identities, and some minor characters have been merged to simplify the plot. The psychiatrist, Dr. Park, for example, actually represents three separate psychiatrists I saw during that time. While the turnover of psychiatric professionals is worth mentioning somewhere, including it in my brief story was deemed too much of a distraction from the main message.

The story begins in December 2013 with a phone call from my therapist, Dr. Rachel, in which I received the bipolar diagnosis. I was thirty-one years old at the time, in a long-time relationship with my partner Susan, and the mother of our then three-year-old child, Skye. As a writer, I toss you right in the middle of this tumultuous time and invite you to join me on this year-long journey through one of the darkest times in my life. In writing this deeply personal book, I don't hold back. My aim is to provide the most accurate depiction of my experiences. I hope to shed light on aspects of serious mental illness and mass trauma that do not receive nearly enough attention. Please note that I share in detail some of the most troubling symptoms of my illness, including suicidal ideation, psychosis, and post-traumatic stress symptoms. The material may be difficult to read, and I therefore urge you to check in on yourself and to practice self-care.

Diagnosis

December 2013

I stepped into the cold with my heart racing and my stomach turning, my red Columbia fleece in contrast with the dark December sky. My ringing phone prompted me to slip out of the holiday party at work. Insecure and introverted, I normally relished in any valid reason to avoid socializing with my colleagues, but this particular call filled me with dread. I answered the phone as the door closed behind me. It was Rachel, my psychologist.

"Hey Ann. I got your message. What's going on?" she asked, her voice cheery as always.

I hurried to the far end of the reflecting pool adjacent to the engineering center. The pool had been emptied for the winter. The benches were empty too, as the students retreated to the warmth of the surrounding buildings. Winter had arrived in full force, and its bitterness gave a chill that raised the hair on my arms. My nose began to drip in the cold air, and my speech was interrupted by intermittent sniffles. I glanced around. No one—yet I spoke softly into the phone.

I inhaled sharply. "Last night, I was in bed, and I couldn't sleep. I figured it was a good time to think about the times I had been manic, like you suggested last time in therapy."

"Yes, of course," she said, seemingly proud that I had taken my homework assignment from therapy seriously. I was a difficult nut to crack, and Rachel was undoubtedly enthusiastic I had taken any of her suggestions seriously. I had landed on her doorstep just weeks prior, battling a variety of emotions that erupted from my failed attempts to get pregnant with a second child. One minute I was raging with anger, shouting hateful things at my partner, Susan. The next minute I was sobbing uncontrollably as "Cat's in the Cradle" played on the car radio. On my eighth intrauterine insemination, or IUI, Susan had given me an ultimatum: "Get help or we are done." I wasn't completely sold on the idea of therapy, but I didn't have a choice. Now, I was reaching out to Rachel because she was the only person who could possibly make sense of what was happening to me.

I continued. "At maybe two o'clock in the morning, a man's voice came from outside my bedroom window and called me 'crazy.'" I didn't know why, but I envisioned the man as a burly, middle-aged man with a ponytail. It was incredibly odd that I could picture him even though I had merely heard his voice. "I looked out the window, but no one was there. I mean, why would someone be outside my bedroom window in the middle of the night? I live in the middle of nowhere. And even if there was a man outside my window, why would he call me crazy?" I swallowed but choked on my saliva. A small cough came from my mouth, the white cloud vanishing before my eyes in the cold air.

"That's a really good point."

"I was thinking about it, and there are times I have seen things that were not there." I paused, not wanting the next words to escape my mouth for fear I had reached a point of no return. I had never shared any of this with anyone before. "One time, I saw a dead body on the side of the road on my way to work. And another time, I saw a man in a demon mask as I walked across campus."

"Okay. And have you ever heard voices before?" Her voice was calm and controlled.

"Not exactly. I mean, sometimes I hear static or ringing. And occasionally I hear whispering, but it's not like I can make out any of the words." I always attributed these things to my overactive imagination, but the problem was the instances were increasing in frequency and severity. I was in trouble. I knew it. I reached out to Rachel for help, foolishly wanting her to tell me everything would be fine. That wasn't going to happen.

"I looked over your intake again when I got your message and based on what you are telling me today, I would give a diagnosis of bipolar disorder with psychotic features." She paused, but I said nothing. "You can learn more about it by searching on the web. Don't read too much though. The information on the internet is not particularly good."

Psychotic. My gut wrenched. The word itself was terrifying. It conjured up images from movies of wild, unpredictable, and violent people who had lost touch with all reality. Was I destined to become the next Jack Torrance from *The Shining*, having conversations with invisible people and plotting to kill my family? I pictured myself running through the streets in my pajamas, talking in code, and screaming hysterically as the cops pulled up.

Psychotic features aside, I had suspected the bipolar diagnosis for years. Depression was self-explanatory—after all, who hadn't experienced a touch of the blues at some time in their life? The opposite pole of mania was a little harder to discern, but if I thought about it, it had been there all along. One spring morning, for example, I had woken up and spontaneously decided to build a bat house. I scoured the internet for blueprints, rushed off to Lowe's to purchase the lumber, and spent two days working nonstop to build a three-chamber bat hotel. I threw my screwdriver to the ground and stormed off when I was unable to hang the bat house. It was too heavy and my ladder too short. I was ill-prepared in my haste. After the mania passed, I gave up on the bat house completely. It sat in my barn collecting dust for a year before I took the initiative to hang it properly on a post in the backyard.

That was how my manias were: spurts of energy and obsessions that lasted for only a few days and then dissolved. Most of my actions were laughable, not problematic. I never had problems with overspending or hypersexuality—weren't those the hallmarks of bipolar disorder? Instead, I was a highly successful professor in one of the top engineering programs in the country. I had a family, owned a house, traveled the world, and lived what I thought to be a happy life. The symptoms I was experiencing in the wake of my battle with infertility were a setback, not a sign of an underlying mood disorder. If I had bipolar disorder, it had to be mild.

"Would you like me to make a referral to a psychiatrist?"

Rachel asked.

The words were sharp as knives. When I initially stepped foot into the taupe-colored house for treatment of depression, anger, and irritability, I told Rachel I wanted to avoid medications. I feared pills would alter my personality and the side effects would ruin my productivity at work. After all, I was hired at the University of Michigan in 2009 as an Assistant Professor "on the tenure track," meaning that I would be granted a permanent position at the university if I could prove myself in the first six years. Now, at the defining moment of my career—Assistant Professor coming up for promotion to Associate Professor with tenure—I faced the very real possibility this illness could ruin my chance of succeeding. It could ruin *everything*—it was not the right time to be experimenting with medications. Not only did I fear loss of productivity, I feared loss of my sense of *self*. Who would I be on medications? What did I stand to lose?

You can't will yourself out of psychosis though.

Still holding the phone, I breathed in the cool air and sat on a bench in the courtyard. The coldness stung the backs of my legs. Stunned, I was unable to respond to Rachel.

"Psychosis is highly treatable with medications," she continued. "I've had a lot of clients who have had success with treatment. We have some really good providers here. I can put in a referral—"

"Go ahead and put in the referral." I sighed.

I knew treatment under a psychiatrist would involve trial and error with medications that came with all kinds of side effects, like weight gain and fatigue. Not only did I dislike the idea of poisoning my body with mind-altering chemicals, but I also had doubts that medications could alleviate the symptoms I was experiencing. The illness, combined with the medication trial, would no doubt affect my productivity at work, and the timing could not have been worse.

"Okay, I will let Dr. Park know." As our call came to an end, she asked, "Any thoughts of hurting yourself or others?"

"No."

"Is there anything else I can do for you today?"

"No, I'm good." I was downplaying the mound of emotions that I felt. The words "bipolar disorder," "psychosis," and "medications" swirled in my head like an oil sheen on water. I was losing my mind, and it seemed there was no turning back. May as well kiss tenure goodbye.

"Do some self-care, okay, hon?"

"Okay."

After the call ended, I slipped the phone into my pocket and climbed the steps to Beal Avenue, drifting in the general direction of my office. Normally on such a cold day, I would have opted for the indoor path made of hallways and hidden stairwells that snaked through the North Campus buildings. However, I stayed outside because the sting of fresh air on my bare face was sobering. My world was crumbling, but the cold brought out the basic signs of life in me. My heart thumped vibrantly, and my lungs inflated and deflated with each piercing breath of chilled air. My head was heavy with the weight of the diagnosis and the impending reality I would need to break the news to Susan in the evening.

As I neared the top of the hill, the voices of two men echoed behind me. It started with some indiscernible chatter and then evolved into laughter. I let out a gasp as my pulse doubled in speed. I closed my eyes, inhaled deeply, and prayed the voices were real. I turned to look over my shoulder and let out a sigh of relief as I observed a couple of college students carrying on a conversation. Real. For a brief moment, a sense of hope and relief came over me—maybe my mind had simply played a trick on me last night.

Back in my office, I obsessively searched the internet for answers, attempting to differentiate between disorders on the psychosis spectrum, reading diagnostic criteria and wondering if they applied to me. From what I could gather, bipolar disorder with psychotic features was the most severe form of bipolar disorder, and, as Rachel had warned, the prognosis was not good. In an attempt to determine what the future would hold, I reflected on my encounters with friends and family who had mental illnesses. The images that came to mind frightened me. Erratic behavior. Crippling depression. Rage. Violence. Suicide.

Breaking the News

December 2013

The Michigan winter sucked me into its abyss with its dismal, charcoal days abbreviated by a blackness that seemingly stretched on forever. The darkness—which fell like a curtain on my evening commute and sustained the absence of light until mid-morning—was suffocating. It was like being trapped deep within a pit with only the narrow beam of my van's headlights to show the way. I drove up the long, gravel driveway in that unending dark, swerving around potholes as the rabbits darted in and out of view like ghosts. I pulled into the garage and took several deep breaths before entering the house.

We lived in a bi-level house, which Susan and I had purchased at the peak of the housing crisis, a time when it was a "buyer's market" and bank foreclosures were abundant. Built in the 1980s, the home had a modern design, including high ceilings and an open-plan layout, but it was in desperate need of repair. The previous owners had neglected the property, and Susan and I couldn't keep up with the perpetually expanding list of things needing attention. When we moved into the house, most of the light fixtures were missing, and the appliances had been sold. The frames of the windows and doors had rotted through, and portions of the cedar siding had suffered water damage from a lack of roof gutters. Humongous, stubborn weeds invaded the garden, leaving it overgrown with spiny gnarls that could not be killed off with even the strongest mix of weed killer. Each year, we crossed a few items off the list, but our efforts were never enough.

Susan and I had been together for twelve years, and over that time, we'd established a partnership founded on love, dedication, and trust. Our evening routine involved one of us playing with our three-year-old, Skye, while the other person prepared dinner. That night after the phone call, it was Susan's night to cook, so I stretched out on the floor to help Skye construct a tower out of blocks. I tried to be in the moment for her sake, extending a hand to balance the blocks as the tower grew, but my thoughts raced and pulled me away, preoccupied with needing to break the news of my bipolar diagnosis to Susan. I was a coward when it came to disrupting the status quo. Avoiding conflict at all costs, I often kept things from her to escape any painful truth. My anxiety left a metallic flavor in my mouth, and my gut rolled and knotted. I couldn't hide my illness forever though and, for one of the few times in my life, I needed a shoulder to cry on. Dinner came and went before I finally mustered up the courage.

"I need to tell you something," I said, as Susan cleared her plate from the dining room table. Dinner was the only time Susan and I were able to talk to one another without interruption. In a moment, one of us would need to break away and get Skye ready for bed. Following that, I would immediately head to bed so I could tend to the morning routine. Skye had already picked through her food and moved into the living room to watch cartoons on her tablet. I emptied Skye's leftovers into the trash, rinsed her plate, and then followed Susan into the living room.

"What is it?" she asked, settling on the couch.

I took a seat next to her, deliberately taking slow breaths.

Susan smiled nonchalantly at me, which eased my fears a little. I had picked up a bottle of wine on my way home from work, hoping it might soften the blow. My head started to swirl like the chardonnay in the glass, signifying it was time to tell her.

I took a deep breath. "Last night, I was having trouble sleeping. I was lying in bed looking up at the ceiling when I heard a man's voice outside of the window say the word 'crazy' to me."

"Wait. What?" She looked at me then, her expression different. One that made the breath catch in my throat.

"I called my therapist today," I hurried on before I lost momentum. "She said it was most likely a hallucination brought on by the bipolar disorder."

"Are you sure you weren't dreaming?"

"No, I was definitely awake."

Susan looked at me with furrowed brows. I hadn't convinced her.

"It's not the first hallucination I think I've had," I continued carefully. "One time I was driving to work and saw a dead body on the side of the road. But when I looked again, there was nothing there."

"Well, that could happen to anyone—"

"And another time there was a man on campus who was wearing a demon-like mask. It couldn't be real."

Susan paused a moment, taking in the bizarre stories I shared.

"If you've been having hallucinations all this time, why didn't you mention it to me earlier?" Her gaze was piercing. The psychosis didn't appear to be the problem, but rather that I had kept something from her. I had violated her trust.

My cheeks reddened. I hadn't intended to be secretive about it, but Susan was right. I should have come to her sooner. In my defense, it was hard to explain the disturbing and sometimes violent images, especially when I did not understand their source. Moreover, for all I knew, everyone saw or heard things that were not there. This was the only perspective I'd ever had. How was my experience any different from the person who thinks she hears the phone ringing when she is in the shower, or the person who sees an object move in the corner of her eye? The mind plays tricks, doesn't it? I figured hearing voices and seeing dead bodies were signs my mind was a little more imaginative than most. I didn't realize these were beyond the limits of what might be considered a normal human experience.

"I didn't know I was having hallucinations." I paused. "Plus, I didn't want to worry you."

As I waited for a reaction, I studied Susan's face. Fine lines were forming around the edges of her eyes like ripples around stones that had broken the still water's surface. Our problems seemed to have become the problems of adults. Perhaps that was what happened when we moved from our twenties to our thirties, when finances became more complex and parenting consumed us. The news I sprang on her would no doubt add to her stress and anxiety. I was supposed to be the one who had it together; I was failing her by losing my mind.

After a long moment, when the words sunk in and the reality left us a little heavier there on the couch, Susan took my hand and calmly said, "We'll deal with this, like everything else we've had to deal with."

A tear escaped the corner of my eye. I sniffled.

"You're going to be okay," she said and hugged me.

Everything was going to be all right. Her reassurance settled over me, warm and comforting. We had been through a lot in our time together and, through all the storms we had weathered, we emerged stronger.

"That means a lot," I said, wiping my eyes. "Thanks for not making a big deal about the hallucination."

"Seriously, you know my family, right?" Susan's family history was rife with mental illness, with conditions as severe as schizophrenia in her bloodline.

"Yeah, I guess you're right."

"We'll get through this. I promise." She squeezed my hand.

"So, the next step is that I need to see a psychiatrist. I don't want to take medications, but I don't think I have any other options. Rachel says psychosis is 'highly treatable.'"

"Whatever it takes." Susan took a sip of her wine, still calm.

"And what if it affects my ability to work?"

"You'll be fine. The side effects are temporary, right?"

"Yeah. You're probably right." I looked down at my wine

glass and rubbed my index finger along the bottom edge of the glass, seeking some form of connection to the present.

"I'll support you in whatever way I can."

Looking up at her, I said, "Thanks. You're the best."

"I know," she said. I smiled and sipped my wine too, emptying the glass.

"Well, I guess I should get this kid to bed." I looked at Skye, who was still engrossed in her cartoons. Blocks speckled the carpet, a tripping hazard for anyone who dared to cross the living room floor. I got her off her tablet, and then she and I tiptoed past the mess, leaving the blocks to be cleaned up another day.

Home

December 2013

"I have a great idea!" I rushed into the bedroom where Susan was folding her clothes. "Let's pack our suitcases in phases! Like, let's pack one for New York, one for Pennsylvania, and one for West Virginia. That way, when we arrive at a destination, we only need to grab one suitcase instead of three." The idea was brilliant.

Susan responded with a flat-out "no." My heart fell, devastated, but only momentarily. It was her way of reeling me back to earth.

I was no doubt edging into mania. We were preparing for our annual trip for the holidays, and this year was a special year because Susan and I were getting married. We had been back and forth on the date, location, and guest list of our wedding for several months. In the end, we decided to elope to Niagara Falls, as we didn't want to be placed in the awkward position of having sent invitations to our closest family only to have them not attend in disapproval. Our family was generally supportive of our relationship, but the concept of same-sex *marriage* pushed the limits.

Over the holiday break, we'd drive from Michigan to

Pennsylvania and leave Skye with my parents. Susan and I would then drive to New York, get married, return to Pennsylvania to celebrate the holidays with my parents, drive to the southernmost part of West Virginia to celebrate the holidays with Susan's family, and finally head home to Michigan. It was a lot to fit into ten days, but we were used to that kind of chaos.

Only a week had passed since my diagnosis. That week, multiple panic attacks left me crying in my car before and after work, at the grocery store, and in the mall bathroom, interrupting our Christmas shopping. I was losing my mind, I was sure, and there was no coming back. I had no concept of how psychosis might progress with time, so I resorted to what I had learned from movies: that psychosis comes on suddenly and cannot be cured. Mania was creeping up on me; fortunately, however, it was a euphoric mania that conveniently coincided with a very important life event: our wedding.

After packing our suitcases and loading up the van, we hit the road. Susan stopped at the toll booth and grabbed a ticket. Then she merged onto the turnpike. "So how are you?" she prompted.

"Good." I opened a Tootsie Roll and popped it in my mouth. "I mean, I guess I'm doing better."

"Any hallucinations?"

"No. I just have a lot of anxiety, like I can't help but feel I'm losing my mind." I paused. "I'm sorry I lost it the other day when we were shopping," I said, referring to the mall panic attack. I ended up having to leave the store and sit in the vehicle while Susan finished the shopping. "The colors were too bright; it was overwhelming."

"I don't think I really understand," she said honestly, "but it's okay."

I tried to put a positive spin on it. "I feel good today though. I've been tracking my moods, and I'm on the upswing. Things will be fine for the wedding." In fact, I was not just feeling good; I was *giddy* and I could hardly contain myself.

"Oh, good." Susan kept her eyes fixed on the road.

I changed the subject and asked Susan about work. Susan was a staff member in a women's center at the University of Michigan-Dearborn campus, which provided students with resources on sexual assault, abuse, homelessness, and more. Susan always had stories to share—she seemed to attract unusual characters and excessive drama. I mostly sat back and listened. Her stories were always so different and interesting compared to mine. The rest of the drive was fairly uneventful.

We arrived at my parents' house just before midnight, the moon reflecting off the fresh snow. As we approached the old farmhouse, a pleasant familiarity greeted me. Over my lifetime, I had seen my family move from poverty to prosperity. Each jump in status was reflected in an upgrade to the old house, and so the house was under constant renovation when I was a child. Carpets pulled up, drywall hung, rooms rewired, walls papered and painted, ditches dug, pipes laid, concrete poured. By the time I reached adulthood, my dad had moved into management at an engineering firm, and my mom taught high school biology. The house was completely made over, but there were still remnants of those early years. Through the process, we learned that, while money did not buy happiness, it certainly made life easier.

Susan parked our van in the snow-covered driveway, and we descended to the house, being careful not to trip on the broken concrete step leading to the patio. Buddy, my parents' English springer spaniel, bounded to greet us at the door. We moved past Buddy through the kitchen and into the dining room, where my mom stood beaming at us. Once all our stuff was in the house, we settled in the living room. My mom liked color, and so every room in the house was a different hue. The paneled walls of the living room had been painted evergreen, making the room seem larger than it was.

"Do you want a beer?" my dad asked with a knowing grin on his face.

"Of course," I said. My dad shuffled down the creaky stairs to the basement, returning with three bottles of his home brew, this time a smooth amber ale. Susan, my dad, and I lifted our bottles in a toast and then each took a sip.

Skye dumped some Hot Wheels cars on the floor and began lining them up along the edge of the coffee table. Buddy settled next to her on the floor, dozing off as if our presence was nothing out of the ordinary. The TV was on, but no one was watching it.

The living room was far warmer than in the days of my childhood. My mind flashed back to the snow that used to gather on the insides of the rotted windows, the warped panes covered in plastic wrap to keep the draft out. The winters were so cold my brothers and I would huddle around the kerosene heater on the living room floor while we watched cartoons on the console TV and played with Legos. Thinking of the kerosene heater reminded me of the blue shag carpet that used to cover the floor. I smiled at the memory.

As I sat there with a beer in hand, fear crept through the nostalgia. I was afraid the conversation would immediately turn to my mental health, as I had told my mom the previous week about the hallucination and the bipolar diagnosis. When I initially told her, I expected some sort of overreaction—a distancing as if it was contagious or sobbing as if I had been diagnosed with a terminal illness—but her response was flattened, as though I'd come down with something as trivial as the common cold. Both of my parents had dealt with depression at various points in their lives, and both had sought medical treatment for it. Depression, anxiety, and substance abuse were not uncommon in my family, but my grandfather was the only member of my family who had been treated for psychosis. No one else in my family had been diagnosed with bipolar disorder. My mom's lack of reaction made it difficult to tell if she merely expected my admission or was in denial.

Instead, we chatted about how things had been with home and work.

"How are Grandma and Grandpap?" I asked.

"They're good. Grandpap fell again the other day. Fortunately, your aunt and uncle were home. They had to go over there and help him up. Grandma's doing good, but her mind is not well. She gets confused sometimes." My mom paused. "As she always said, it's hell to get old."

My dad changed the subject. "Hey Annie, how's work?" His background in electrical engineering made him the only person in my entire family who really understood what I did for a living.

I was slightly put off by the question. My productivity had slipped in recent months due to the deterioration of my mental health. On the days I was depressed, I did nothing but sleep. When I was not depressed, either I was so irritable I could hardly contain myself, or my mind was moving so quickly I could not focus on any one thing. In addition, I had been beating myself up over the new diagnosis, feeling weak for allowing the illness to happen in the first place. Even though I was struggling, I could not let on I was barely keeping afloat. After all, I was the straight-A kid who grew up to be a professor at the elite University of Michigan, not the kind of person who succumbed to an illness like bipolar disorder.

"It's okay. Teaching went well this semester. I got four point nine out of five on my course evaluations," I tried to keep my voice level. "Right now, I'm busy trying to get papers submitted, you know, with tenure coming up and all."

"How do you feel about tenure?"

"I'm nervous," I admitted. "My colleagues keep telling me I'm going to be fine, but I'm not so sure. My funding is okay, but I need more papers." I paused, feeling the shame that I was blowing my one chance of success. I shuddered at the thought, and then I tried to recover. "I guess everyone is worried when they come up for tenure, though."

"Yeah, that makes sense," he said.

My mom changed the topic. "Are you ready for the wedding?"

"Yeah," I said. I could hardly wait to drive to Canada in the morning. Not only was the wedding *finally* happening, but it was going to be the first trip Susan and I had made alone since Skye's birth. "I mean, it's not a big, extravagant wedding or anything. We are just going to the courthouse for the ceremony. We'll be staying in Canada, which will be nice. I don't expect there will be many people there this time of year."

"I wish I could go with you." My mom pouted a little. It was hard to tell if her reaction was genuine. While she had disapproved of Susan when she initially met her, my mom eventually came around and welcomed Susan into the family. I tried not to freeze my mom in time, but it was hard to forget that there was a time when my parents were not hugely supportive of my being queer.

"But mom, we couldn't invite family because we weren't sure who would attend. How awful would it be if we invited family and they didn't attend in disapproval? We didn't want any feelings to be hurt."

"I know. But I wish I could be there."

"Me too," I responded, although Susan and I both knew it was best to have none of our family present at the wedding. We had learned early on it was best to keep our affection concealed. Something as minor as a leg across a lap while lounging on the couch had forced us out of a relative's house a few years prior. It only took that one instance before Susan and I understood we needed to be discreet. While we maintained overall good relationships with our parents, having family at the wedding would only cause Susan and me to act unnaturally distant from each other, and that was not a feeling we deserved on our wedding day.

The friction in our relationships with our parents was unsettling to me. When I was a child, life with my family was simple and perfect in every way. I was given the freedom to explore the world on my own, with gentle guidance when I began veering down the wrong path. My parents instilled in me the values of honesty, hard work, education, and independence. In my eyes, growing up in the idyllic family, it seemed they were model parents.

But when I left home, my parents' shortcomings were magnified by my new understanding of the world. They were no longer the experts in everything; rather, their knowledge was constrained by their limited life experiences. I no longer looked to my parents for advice on most things, and the advice I did receive was taken at face value. Relationships became complicated as my brothers and I moved out of state and started families of our own. As the family grew to include in-laws and children, things became unnecessarily complex. I didn't fully understand it, but a part of me longed for the days when it was just my parents, my brothers, and me.

I looked at the family photo collage hanging above the loveseat. For their thirty-fifth wedding anniversary, my mom and dad rented a beach house and invited my brothers and me to bring our families for a weeklong vacation in South Carolina. It was the first time my brothers and I had been under the same roof in years. I was thrilled at the idea of reuniting with them, but once we arrived at the beach house, the tensions became unbearable. The fact was that my brothers and I had formed our own families and established our own values—that we had grown our own families in our own ways—and our expansion meant we no longer fit under one roof with my parents, not even for a single week's duration. In the photos, we appeared happy in our myriad of teal shirts as we posed in various arrangements on the sunlit beach. However, hidden behind those photos was the truth our family would never again be what it was when we were kids. I shuddered and turned my gaze from the collage.

We finished our beers over a lighter conversation, until my mom eventually said, "Well, you should probably get Skye to bed."

"Yeah, we have a long drive ahead of us tomorrow." I knelt by Skye and helped her clean up her toys.

The Wedding

December 2013

The sun was nearly set by the time Susan and I arrived in the fog-enclosed ghost town of Niagara Falls. On the eve of winter, the touristy areas had been abandoned like a carnival after hours. Novelty shops and nightclubs glittered, but the town was largely devoid of people. As much as I hated crowds, the lack of people was a satisfying discovery, and the flashy lights added an excitement that was befitting of our nontraditional wedding.

It is important to note Niagara Falls was an ironic symbol of my love for Susan. More than a decade ago, we visited the falls with a group of friends, thrilled at the idea of legally being able to drink across the Canadian border at the age of nineteen. I ended up being kicked out of a nightclub for showing affection toward Susan at a time when being queer was less acceptable than today. The bouncer tapped me on the shoulder, told me I had too much to drink, and kicked me to the curb. Getting married in a place where we had experienced such intolerance gave me an odd feeling of satisfaction.

Susan and I had a dramatic beginning, befitting any work of fiction. I had just finished my freshman year in college when I joined my friends for summer work at Cedar Point, an amusement park on Lake Erie. My friends and I were assigned to a three-bedroom employee apartment arranged to sleep eight people, and of course, as fate would have it, Susan and I were roommates. On the day I met her, Susan literally leaped over the couch to greet me and then dragged me to the fridge to show off her newly hung poster of supermodel Carmen Electra, who was dressed in a bikini and posing against the surf. Susan was the first person I had met who was openly (and unapologetically) gay. Over the next few months, we spent every waking moment together, and by the end of summer, our relationship had evolved into something more than just a friendship.

I was drawn to Susan mostly because we were complete opposites. Whereas my social interactions were awkward and riddled with anxiety, Susan was fearless and bold, always quick to a joke that made the room reel with laughter. She was an all-star athlete in high school—captain of the cross-country team and slated to be captain of the cheerleading squad. After high school, she was *alive*. Not knowing her purpose, she followed her intuition and leaped from opportunity to opportunity. Pressured by her family to pursue factory work, Susan drove to Cedar Point for summer work only because a stranger she had met on the internet was planning to do it. Rather than settling for the traditional life her family had planned out, she had gone to a strange place to party with even stranger people. I was drawn to Susan because everything she did was rooted in her core beliefs, which never wavered. She was a champion for women's rights, Black rights, gay rights, and more, and she didn't hesitate to challenge my ways of thinking. She was strange and complex, and there was a depth to her personality that took me years to uncover. Above all, I loved her because she was the only person I had ever met who brought out the hidden aspects of my personality I never knew existed.

Despite our closeness, we never attempted to define ourselves as being anything more than friends. At the time, I was drawn to Susan, but in a way I had never felt with anyone ever before. I got butterflies in my stomach when we were close, and I went out of my way to impress her. One bright morning before the park opened, I met Susan at the rollercoaster she operated and surprised her with flowers I had handpicked along the way. We weren't officially a couple, but that small act felt right. I didn't know where Susan stood though; any time the topic of relationships came up, Susan was rather vocal about not wanting to be in a long-term relationship with anyone—ever. By the end of the summer, we went our separate ways—Susan to Indiana and I to Pennsylvania—although we communicated regularly by email.

When she was gone, I isolated myself in the bedroom of my college apartment and obsessively wrote in my journal, piecing together a distorted perception of what had actually happened that summer, yearning for that connection with Susan again and the joy it had brought me. Then, in a moment of desperation, I mailed a letter to her stating how I truly felt about her, that I loved her and could not stand the thought of losing her. It took her three months to respond—three agonizing months during which I kicked myself relentlessly for exposing my feelings in such a stupid and childish manner—but one December evening she called to tell me she felt the same way about me. I convinced her to move to Pittsburgh, and that was the official start to our relationship.

It was painfully unfair that Susan and I could not have a traditional wedding like most couples because our families didn't give us clear signals of support. However, we weren't passionate newlyweds, driven to marriage by blind faith, with hopes we would beat the odds of divorce. Instead, our relationship was a spectacular canyon carved by torrential rains that had come and gone over centuries. Our exteriors had been washed away, layer by layer, until the colors beneath became exposed. You could make out every twist and turn we had made, two ledges, side by side, navigating life's obstacles as one. We had been built to withstand the most extreme circumstances and to stand for eternity. As a same-sex couple, we had waited years in anticipation of the day we could marry. For us, marriage was not only a public declaration of our love. It meant the kind of security that can only come with the recognition our collection of three individuals living as one household was indeed a family.

"How do I look?" Susan asked as she stepped into the room.

"Beautiful!" I exclaimed. She was wearing a white lace dress cut just above the knee, a belt around her waist, and brown leather boots. Her medium-brown hair, which was once hopelessly straight, had developed a soft wave following her pregnancy with Skye. In the low light of the hotel room, her skin shimmered like moonlight on a tranquil lake on a clear summer night. I was reminded of the time many years ago we had shared a hotel room in Cleveland, the first time Susan casually folded her arm across my waist as she slept soundly, the night I lay awake listening to her breathing, feeling her heartbeat, and hoping the sun would never come. On our wedding day, in that moment, as she stood before me in that dress, it was as if I was seeing her for the first time. My stomach fluttered with excitement as I looked into the two blue eyes gazing back at me. They were the same eyes I had looked into ten thousand times, the same eyes that had seen me through raging storms and endless blue skies, the eyes that were steadfast, my anchors to earth.

"You don't look too bad yourself," she said playfully. I was much less stunning in my tan suit, but it didn't matter.

She began to gather her things. "If we leave now, we'll have plenty of time to eat before picking up the flowers and heading to City Hall."

"We'll have to eat somewhere that's quick. I don't want to be late." It was the usual anxiety that drove me to be overly punctual.

"There's a Denny's near the florist. That'll be fast."

I didn't know what other couples eat on their wedding day, but I imagined the meals would be decided upon with the utmost care. It might seem that Denny's would be a poor choice for such a special day, especially since our newly earned upper-middle class had brought with it wholesome, organic foods and snobbery towards anything fried. But for Susan and me, dining at Denny's on our wedding day was a sort of tribute to our days of living below the poverty line. I could not even count the hours we had spent sitting in diners with barely enough cash to buy a meal. No matter how wealthy we had become, there would always be days when fries and cheap diner coffee tasted just right.

It started to drizzle, and the damp air blew over us as we walked from the van to the restaurant. I wiped my brow with the back of my hand as we stepped inside. The hostess sat us in a booth facing the parking lot. The restaurant was otherwise empty.

"You know, I can't even remember the last time we ate at a Denny's," Susan said.

"I can. Remember the one at Lake Powell? The day before you proposed to me."

"Oh yeah! You're right." She paused for a moment of reflection. "That was such a fun trip."

I smiled as I glanced down at the engagement ring I would now wear on my right hand. It was a simple ring—a white-gold band clasping five small diamonds. Susan had bought it for me five years prior when we were struggling as students to make ends meet. After trekking through miles of Arizona desert by car and by foot, we rented a kayak and paddled across Lake Powell for a bagged lunch. When we finished eating—on the most pristine day amongst the red and white walls of the lake with not a soul as a witness—Susan surprised me with the ring. At the time, I had accepted marriage was something I would never see in my lifetime. Receiving an engagement ring gave me hope for something more.

"We've done a lot, haven't we?" I said as I looked back over our life together. Our wild sense of adventure had taken us to random and exotic places, leaving us with so many memories. Like the time we had almost been eaten by lions while on safari in South Africa. Or the time we had raced to the coast to see the final launch of the Atlantis Space Shuttle. We had done L.A. in a day, Paris and Zurich in a week. We had hiked alongside wild ponies in Appalachia, climbed sand dunes over Lake Michigan, and stood in vortices in Sedona. We lived for the extreme. It was exhausting at times, but neither of us could deny we lived life to the fullest.

Over the next half hour, we scarfed down fries and gulped our coffees. The conversation flowed like a faucet cleared of debris. It was the first time we had been away from Skye for an extended time, and we were without the usual stresses of work and parenting. The responsibility that came with adulthood had stifled our relationship. Yet at that moment we were kids again, rediscovering our love for each other and uncovering our true selves in the process. Our life no doubt moved at a slower pace these days, but we were without regret. Skye gave my life purpose, and Susan gave me strength and courage.

To my relief, we arrived at City Hall with time to spare. We found a metered spot on the street to park, and then we climbed the steps to the entrance. The inside of the building had the cold, everlasting feel of granite, which gave me a brief moment of hesitation. I expected the usual judgmental stares, like the kind we received when entering a restaurant in any rural American town. However, the people inside the City Hall greeted us with smiles and kind words. The outpouring of support was a pleasant surprise, one that allowed me to relax my shoulders and breathe easier.

The room we were wed in was large, with pale blue walls and fern-green carpeting. It was like being trapped in a time capsule from the 1970s, the room's yellowed fluorescent lights and its scent of church pews. The wedding ceremony that followed was simple, intimate, and beautiful, perfect in every way for the two of us. Yet, as Susan and I declared our vows, the words "in sickness and in health" resounded in my mind, echoing the fears I held deep inside that I was rapidly losing my mind. I quickly brushed the fears aside as I stepped into Susan's embrace.

"I now pronounce you *together* for life," the officiant proclaimed. We sealed the marriage with a kiss.

The following day, we returned to Pennsylvania where we reunited with Skye. We diligently followed our plan, staying with my parents for a couple of days before heading to West Virginia and then returning home. Following the mania, my mood predictably evolved into a depression in which I became lethargic and ill-tempered. My sleep was fractured, and my migraines and asthma flared up under the stress of travel. The words "in sickness and in health" reverberated in my mind, a constant reminder that I was slipping into madness.

Being away from work, I had time for reflection. I questioned whether I really had bipolar disorder, as the symptoms of the illness were surreal. *Surely I didn't hear a voice. Susan is right. I* must've *been dreaming*, I told myself. It was as if I was plagued by some sort of amnesia that prevented me from remembering what I had experienced. I spent time digging deep into my past, trying to piece together the roots of my illness, and I read as much as I could about the disorder.

Coming up on the new year, I was optimistic things were going to get better. Our attempts to get pregnant would be put on hold, and I would be starting treatment for my bipolar disorder. I would finally be able to get back to the real me, to put this raging monster behind me. As the darkness fell in the last few hours of 2013, Susan and I prepared our traditional New Year's Eve meal, dubbed "appetizer surprise," a dinner of mozzarella sticks, vegetarian chicken wings, waffle fries, and the like that we would eat from a lazy Susan my mom had bought us the previous Christmas. My mom *swore* the name "lazy Susan" was purely coincidental.

I sat in the living room playing cars with Skye while Susan checked on the food baking in the oven. Without warning, Susan's voice came at full volume from the kitchen. "Ann, come here quick! The handle to the oven, it—it fell off!"

Disturbed by the alarm in her voice, I leaped from the couch. "What do you mean?" I asked as I turned the corner into the kitchen. I looked down to find the left side of the handle completely unscrewed and dangling from the front of the oven door. I ran to grab a screwdriver and started at it, holding the door firmly and attempting to tighten the screw. Not a second later, the glass front of the door completely shattered. Glass exploded into a million jagged beads that popped and crackled in the floor, slicing dozens of tiny red cuts into the palms of my hands. Stunned, I dusted the glass from my palms, grabbed a broom, and told Susan to take Skye into the back bedroom so I could clean up the enormous mess.

That was the start to 2014.

The Psychiatrist

January 2014

In the winter of 2014, our town became a world of darkness and ice. We experienced record snowfalls in southeast Michigan, with totals hovering around one hundred inches. The first major snowstorm of the season arrived early in January, and a steady stream of snow continued through April. Every time I looked out the window and saw more white, my heart skipped a beat. Snow made me anxious because I was the one responsible for clearing the one-thousand-foot driveway leading to our home. Despite having a truck with a plow, I was pathetic when it came to snow removal, and my inadequacies became embarrassingly apparent that winter. The unending snowfall and drifting made it impossible to maintain a navigable pathway from the road to our house. Our vehicles were frequently almost buried by the apparent avalanche—their tires digging deep, stuck in the snow. At one point we were parking the minivan at the end of the driveway as our only means of escape, with both the car and plow truck fatally trapped between the house and the road. Many days that winter, I trudged down the driveway in subzero temperatures to reach the van, the snow deep enough that it reached Skye's waist and the brutal wind burning our faces.

That winter, I was filled with anger and frustration, creating a toxic environment at home. My bipolar disorder had a way of tinging benign words with hate; some sort of mental filter distorted the neutral tones of others, making it seem like I was constantly berated. I became extremely irritable with fire pumping through my veins, igniting every fiber of my being with hatred. When I got like that, I would act out in ways totally uncharacteristic of me, for example, putting my fist through the wall, leaving my knuckles swollen and covered in blood, or marching out the door barefooted in the midst of a thunderstorm, wandering the streets of my neighborhood while the lightning flashed and my feet became serrated from the asphalt pavement. That winter, I frequently lashed out at Susan for what seemed like no apparent reason.

"Did you take out the trash?" she asked harmlessly.

"*Yes*, I took out the trash."

"You don't have to yell at me."

"*I'm not yelling!*" The flames scorched my lungs and drove me out into the snow, slamming the door behind me.

Susan felt she walked on eggshells when I got like that. At the time, I could not understand why, as I was normally very kind and soft-spoken.

My only coping mechanism was to turn my energy toward something productive before things got out of hand. The snow gave me a safe space to take out my rage and expend my seemingly endless energy. I would catch myself yelling in anger, pause, walk out the door with shovel in hand, and hammer away at the snow for hours. When there was no snow to shovel, I jumped on the treadmill. Physical exertion was the only cure to my madness, although the calm that followed was, unfortunately, only short-lived.

That January, following the diagnosis I received from Rachel, I made an appointment with a psychiatrist, who would do a formal evaluation and determine an appropriate medication regimen. I set off for that appointment on a blustery Saturday morning. The babysitter, who had nearly wrecked her car on the way over, warned me the roads were slick.

"It'll be okay," I said. "I'm pretty good at driving in winter weather."

"If you say so." She took a seat on the floor to play with Skye.

I made it down the driveway without trouble and reached the dirt road. A light rain coated the densely packed snow, creating a slick sheet of ice. As I pulled out of the driveway, my van turned the dance of a figure skater in slow motion, circling a complete three hundred and sixty degrees before coming to a stop. Missing the bank and determined to make my appointment, I continued past the half dozen cars that had veered off the road. I turned onto the paved road, which was salted and clear, and drove to Ann Arbor at a pace slower than the usual seventy miles per hour.

Despite my slow start, I arrived on time. Nonetheless, I felt like I might throw up from the dread of being there. My mom once made me see a psychiatrist when I was a teenager. She walked into my room one day and announced she and my dad were "concerned" about my recent behaviors and thought it was best if I "talked to someone." At the time, I spent nearly every waking hour holed up in my bedroom, the curtains drawn and dark music blaring from my radio. When I did leave my room, I was on my way out the door to catch a ride with a friend on my way to drink (or drug) my problems away. Only brief words were exchanged between me and my parents, and any prodding about what I was up to resulted in a teenage sneer. There was no doubt I was depressed at the time, but I could not let my parents know my experimentation with hallucinogens and ecstasy was the root of my depression, or so I thought. That evening, at a time after dark when most doctors' offices were closed, my parents brought me to see a middle-aged man with a beard and glasses who pretended to be someone a sixteen-year-old girl could warm up to. I don't remember what he was wearing, but my imagination leads me to believe he was dressed in a sweater and slacks. He took me back to his office alone and asked me a series of personal questions. *Was I happy? Did I have friends? What was my home life like? How was school going? Did I ever feel down? How often?* I resisted interacting with him, giving one-word answers when possible and lying in response to any question that might show I was anything other than a normal teenager. After one or two appointments, he declared me mentally healthy, and I never went back.

That first psychiatrist fit a stereotype. He gave off a Freudian vibe, and I could feel him deconstructing my personality, trying to figure out what piece of my childhood led to me being so screwed up. To seek out Rachel, even twenty years later, was a stretch. Seeing a psychiatrist as an adult and exploring psychiatric medications were like teetering on the edge of a cliff.

I leafed to a clean page in my journal so I could reflect on starting medications. Taking psychiatric medications, I thought, might change a person's character, making them someone they really are not. Antidepressants, said the media (and reinforced by countless friends and family members), were "happy pills," which rid a person of sadness. It made me wonder, is the person on antidepressants still the *same person*? I looked to my parents, who had taken antidepressants at various points in their lives. When they were on medications, I noticed the change in their mood. Yet I was never sure they were the same people as before. I had to conclude that people resorted to medications because they were weak. I was stronger than my parents, I thought. I always felt that if I toughed it out, there would be no need to manage my moods with medications. And that supposedly worked well for me, at least up to that point.

It seemed psychosis, though, was a different beast altogether. I had pushed my way through the darkest depressions most of my life. However, I had no clue how to handle the psychosis. More and more, I was unable to wish the voices and images and paranoia away. It was utterly frightening each and every time it happened. As I sat in the psychiatrist's waiting room, my gut burned with the reality that medications were my only option.

The clock ticked its way to four minutes past my scheduled appointment. A man in his mid-twenties emerged from a room down the hallway. With his eyes to the floor, he walked swiftly through the waiting room, jogged up the steps, and exited to the parking lot, the door slamming in his wake. A moment later, an Asian-American woman in a black North Face fleece stepped into the waiting room. She was no older than I was.

"Ann?" she called. I was the only person in the waiting room.

I jumped from my chair, gave an awkward smile, and then pointed my eyes to the floor.

Probably sensing my nervousness, she said warmly, "It's so nice to meet you. Come on in."

I took a seat as Dr. Park closed the door. The office had a temporary feel to it as if she had moved in for the day. There were no books or papers aside from the file she had pulled from the front office. She did not even have a computer in front of her.

"So how are things going?" she said with a look of concern.

I let out a nervous laugh. "Ah, it's okay." I paused and then corrected myself. "I mean, it's been better."

"Tell me a little more about what's going on."

I took a deep breath and dove into my story.

By the time I arrived in Dr. Park's office, I had already exhaustively researched bipolar disorder. I entered my appointment armed with the mounting evidence of my illness: the mood chart I had been keeping for several weeks and the journal I had begun using to jot down my erratic thoughts and feelings. I knew the diagnostic criteria, and I had an idea of where my illness fit. Given how successful I was professionally, it was pretty clear to me my bipolar disorder was mild, if anything. I ignored all the research that said bipolar disorder with psychotic features was the most severe form of the illness. After all, I could not think of a time I had been fully manic, and I had never been hospitalized. If it was not for the psychotic features, I would not have sought medications at all. As I talked, Dr. Park feverishly scribbled notes. Occasionally, she interrupted with a question that dug further at my symptoms. We explored all aspects of my work and home life, and I detailed my extensive family history. After nearly thirty minutes of listening, she confirmed the bipolar diagnosis.

"It sounds like you are experiencing a combination of mania and depression, which is what we call a mixed episode. I'm going to prescribe an atypical antipsychotic medication to bring you out of the mania."

Antipsychotic. Psychotic. Psycho.

The words rang in my mind like the tone of a large brass bell. I sat there stunned as the echo resonated. I had little formal training when it came to mental illness. The rest of my understanding came from what I had absorbed from the media, which generally displayed exaggerated, and often inaccurate, perceptions of persons with mental illness, especially when it came to the topic of psychosis. The words were synonymous, weren't they? Psychotic, psychopath.

"We will see how you do on the antipsychotic medication before we add a mood stabilizer," she said. "For a mood stabilizer, I'd like to start with Lamictal. It tends to have fewer side effects than Lithium. Plus, you don't have to get all the bloodwork that would be needed with Lithium."

Dr. Park explained some things related to the medication that seemed important, but I was too dumbfounded to follow her words. I could only absorb clips and phrases. *Take the medication in morning. Do not miss a dose. Dizziness. Nausea. Weight gain. Bloodwork. Sign this form. Come back in a week.*

In the parking lot, I stared at the slips of paper Dr. Park had handed me. The confirmation of the diagnosis by a second doctor brought with it a grave finality. It was as if the gavel had fallen. And my verdict came with a life sentence. A lifetime of illness without a cure, one which brought isolation, shame, and an endless supply of medication to numb my being. Sure, I had had symptoms of bipolar disorder for as long as I could remember. And looking back now, I could also see symptoms of psychosis at various points in my life. The paranoia, the distorted thinking, the startling images, the occasional voice—they had been there since I was a teenager. However, I never had a name for it. Knowing it was psychosis changed the game completely. It was only a matter of time before I'd be locked up on the psych ward in a hospital gown with the rest of the psychotic people.

In what seemed a whirlwind of an experience at Dr. Park's office, I found myself climbing into my van and starting the engine. I'd get my prescription filled before returning home to Skye. I drove down the highway, stunned, and, sitting in the parking lot, I again stared at the slips of paper for nearly ten minutes before working up the courage to walk inside the pharmacy. Stepping through those doors meant I was entering a strange new territory and I'd never be able to come back to the life I had known. Mood or personality, either way, I was going to be changed forever under my new medications.

With a deep breath, I climbed out of the van, skirted through the sliding doors, and bee-lined it to the back of the store. As discreetly as possible, I slid the prescriptions across the counter to the pharmacy technician, being careful to avoid eye contact. My face burned red with embarrassment. It is now public knowledge, I thought. I am certifiably crazy.

The technician, however, gave no reaction—no smirk, no widening of the eyes, not even a raising of the eyebrow. She entered the prescription into the system after verifying my name and birthdate and told me to wait fifteen minutes. Perhaps the antipsychotic medication was not such a big deal.

The Demon

January 2014

I jumped from my bed as though it was the first day of school. I rushed toward the kitchen to make my morning coffee and then grabbed the packaging that held my precious new medication: Geodon. After tearing the bag open, I found a small bottle with exactly thirty pills—one month's supply—of my first antipsychotic medication. Glued to the bottle was a thick manual that must have been a hundred tiny pages of single-spaced text in four-point font. I flipped through the manual, attempted to read a few pages, and then tossed it aside once I came to sketches of molecules representing the drug compound.

"I don't have time for this." I threw the manual into the trash can. I opened the childproof lid, stabbed the protective foil covering the opening to the bottle, and poured one small, white capsule into my hand.

As I stared at the pill, my mind returned briefly to the manual I had just thrown in the trash. *This medication is for the treatment of schizophrenia.* While I had skimmed further to see that, indeed, the medication was also indicated for the treatment of bipolar disorder, my mind was stuck on the word "schizophrenia." I pushed back the stereotypes that spun around my head, placed the pill on my tongue, and downed it with a sip of water.

Things were finally going to get better for me. I was eager for my moods to return to normal and, of course, my bipolar disorder to be miraculously cured. Not long after filling my prescription the day before, I resigned myself to the fact that it didn't matter whether my mood or personality changed; all that mattered was getting these hallucinations out of my life. I was optimistic for a good thirty minutes. Then I felt like I was going to vomit. I pursed my lips together and traced the wall with my hand to find my way to the couch. The world spun and swayed, and all I could do was grip the sofa tightly, my face planted between the cushions. I let out a moan.

Susan, who sat across from me on the loveseat, looked up from her phone.

"Everything okay?" Her eyebrow was raised curiously.

I moaned again. "No." Then, dramatically, "I think I'm dying."

"Do you need to go to the hospital?" I could not tell if she said this because she was seriously worried about me or if she was merely calling my bluff. Susan didn't put up with nonsense from anyone, not even me. Dying, I supposed, was probably an overstatement.

"No. I'll be fine." I huffed a breath of air. "I've just never felt so terrible before."

"Why don't you go and lie down?"

Feeling bad that I was ruining the start of a perfectly good Sunday, I collected myself from the couch, staggered down the hallway, and flung myself onto the bed. I thought about asking Susan to bring me a bucket in case I needed to throw up, but I decided not to because I did not want her to see me as weak. It was just a tiny pill, after all. I pulled the pillow over my head and writhed with abdominal pain and nausea, waiting for the medication to wear off. I tossed and turned like a child with a fever, my body unable to find reprieve.

After an hour or so, I heard noises from the kitchen signaling lunch was almost ready. I felt well enough to climb out of bed and take a shower. Susan and Skye finished eating as I entered the room.

"Look who it is," Susan said. "Feel any better?"

"Yeah, I do. Man, that was awful."

I sat at the table with my plate of scrambled tofu and hash browns. It was our vegan version of an American brunch. I sprinkled my food with salt and looked to see Susan's and Skye's plates smeared with ketchup.

"How do you feel about going to a women's basketball game this afternoon?" she asked.

I took a bite of tofu.

"I mean, if you don't feel like it—"

"No, I'm fine now. Let's go. It'll be fun," I said. I didn't really enjoy going to the university basketball games, but I didn't want to let Susan and Skye down.

"You hear that, Skye? We're going to a basketball game," she said.

"Yay! Go Blue!" As a three-year-old, Skye hadn't yet been conditioned by society to favor men's sports over women's. I was glad for that.

After lunch, we headed to Ann Arbor. As we drove, I stared out the car window in silence. This was going to be a lot harder than I had thought. I had heard side effects were common with psychiatric medications, but I had never experienced anything so awful as the dizziness and nausea from that morning. Dr. Park had said it would take at least a week before I would start to see the effects of the medication, and that there would be side effects the first few days, which should lessen with time. I hoped the side effects didn't last long; I wasn't sure I could tolerate any more of what I had experienced that morning.

The following morning, almost as soon as the pill slid down into my stomach, I was struck with the same unbearable feeling, the abdominal pain and nausea that had plagued me the previous day. I was ill by the time I arrived on campus, and I spent the better part of the morning writhing on the floor of my office. Fortunately, I didn't have any meetings scheduled and just missed a morning of research. The next day, I tried taking the medication at four o'clock in the morning so I might sleep through the dizziness and nausea before having to get ready for work. However, that plan failed too. I couldn't go back to sleep. I didn't have to roll around the floor once I got to work, but waking up at four o'clock every morning was unsustainable.

I didn't notice an improvement in my mood initially, but somewhere around the fourth day my mood improved dramatically. I was cured. I felt alive for the first time in what seemed a very long time. I walked the hallways on campus with an extra bounce in my step, and I was uncharacteristically outgoing towards students and colleagues. My mind was clear, and my sense of humor had returned. It was as if the clouds had parted, letting rays of white light illuminate the world around me. Everything in my surroundings seemed to shimmer with golden effervescence.

But it was far too good to be true. I had a laser-sharp focus and an over-the-top joy that could only come from the intoxicating chemicals flooding my brain. It was the kind of high that was alluring, a sort of natural drunkenness a person with bipolar disorder was predisposed to. It was the exact definition of mania.

In the evening, Susan drove me to the pharmacy to sort out my prescription. In addition to my antipsychotic medication, the pharmacy sent me home with someone else's antidepressant. It was the first of many mix-ups the pharmacy would make. Incongruent to my anger at the pharmacy's carelessness, I was elated and full of energy.

We drove along our dirt road toward town. Susan talked about her day at work, but I couldn't register the meaning of her words. It was as if there were too many stimuli in our surroundings, making it impossible for me to grasp what came out of her mouth. My eyes darted in all directions, seeking to catalog each and every contour and texture outside the car. My mind took snapshots with every glance, storing the beautiful images for when the world would undoubtedly become gray and bland again. Silky snow. Jagged bark. Rubbery power line. Smiling house. Ominous demon—

A demon—a real, live *demon*—skulked in the shadows on the side of the road. A dark creature with the body of an insect, horns protruding from its pentagon-shaped head. Its four legs were jagged and bent, its body elongated like a praying mantis. Sinister eyes slanted in malice pointed directly at me. The demon zigzagged in the sky and then disappeared from view.

"Can you believe she did that?" Susan asked.

I shook my head and squinted my eyes, looking around to see where the demon went.

"Huh?" I asked senselessly. Then, realizing Susan was in the midst of a story I had not been following, I quickly corrected myself. "I mean, no. That's ridiculous."

Susan continued to tell her story. I looked out the window for the demon.

I realized I should have been alarmed by its presence. It was, without question, a visual hallucination. I knew in the moment it was not real, yet, to see such a frightening creature, I was not fearful. Instead, I became even more euphoric. I had an energy that couldn't be tamed and a smile permanently fixed to my face.

"Hey, how much will you pay me to make a scene at the pharmacy? Like, I should go in there and throw the bottle of pills at the pharmacy technician and say, 'I demand my money back!'" I said.

Susan laughed. "Yeah, I can really see *you* doing that."

"No really, I'm going to go in there and start shouting. 'I'm reporting you to corporate,' or something like that." I let out a side-splitting laugh.

The idea of me throwing a fit in the pharmacy tickled me. When we arrived at the pharmacy, I struggled to suppress my giggles as I explained the situation to the pharmacist. I received an apology and was paid off with a twenty-dollar gift card.

I got back in the van.

"How did they know that a twenty-dollar gift card was exactly what I needed to keep me from reporting them?" I asked Susan.

"That's how they handled it? Oh my."

"And I really made a scene too."

"You did?"

"No, not really. But I should've." I was in a *great* mood, and I couldn't be contained. I wanted to run and shout and jump and swing and fly. I wanted to move and to move *fast*. I wanted to be loud. I wanted to wander through the night and look at the beauty of nature. And I wanted to savor *every last minute* of it because a euphoric mania is truly a gift.

But I did none of those things. Instead, we drove towards home. I continued in my silliness, spouting off jokes and laughing. Susan played along.

"This is so much fun! Let's drive around the block. I'm not ready to go home yet," I said.

I gazed out the window at the snow-covered darkness. Colorful holiday lights illuminated the houses in the distance. The world was cartoon-like, with everything defined by sharp boundaries and brilliant colors. I felt alive, like a starburst galaxy in the midst of rapidly forming a new star, and I was absolutely going to explode if I had to hold it in any longer. We drove down Pottery Road and came upon a large white house that had several red barns and sheds on the property.

"Did you ever notice how many barns they have at that house? I mean, what could they possibly use them for?" I paused for a moment, and then it came to me. "We should call it 'Pottery Barns'!" I joked, referencing the home goods store. Susan laughed, and I was the star of a stand-up comedy routine.

"Hey, we should do this all the time," I said. It was as if driving around at night was the most thrilling thing we could ever do.

Susan chuckled, but then she glanced at me, and her expression grew serious. "You're being kind of weird tonight."

"What do you mean?" I asked, still half in giggles.

"You're just kind of...off."

I laughed. "I'm just in a really good mood."

Over the next few days, I had to fight to fall asleep. I would awaken at odd hours of the night, wide-eyed and ready to begin the day. Despite the lack of sleep, I had more energy than ever. But the euphoria didn't last. Instead, my mood darkened. My head filled with a sickening sensation like the kind of embarrassment I felt when I believed people were making fun of me behind my back. It was the feeling of eyes peering at me amid whispers and snickers. Except I was having that feeling when no one was criticizing me but myself. Every flaw and every weakness was brought to light for all the world to see. My skin began to crawl, and an incessant burning filled my chest, a deep hollowness in my gut. My mind kept telling me how worthless I was, how much of a failure I was, how the world would be a better place without me in it. All I wanted to do was curl into a ball and disappear. The feeling continued that way for days with no relief. It took only a few days to reach the end of my rope. I wanted to die.

One morning, after Susan walked out the door, I peeled myself off the couch and headed to the bathroom to get ready for work. I stepped into the shower and ran the warm water over my face in an attempt to wash away that unbearable feeling, but even the calm of the shower couldn't help. At that moment, an overwhelming desire broke into my head. I looked at my razor. I wanted it against my skin. My heart raced as my veins raised to the surface, pulling toward the razor like metal to a magnet. I imagined the sting as the blade sliced my flesh, the blood trickling towards the drain in thin red streaks.

I shook my head. "No, this is not me."

I turned off the water, hurried out of the shower, and drove to work.

The disturbing scene that had played out in my mind left me startled. The imagery had been so real it was palpable. It was not the first time something like that had happened to me, but this time the feeling was unusually strong. I knew I was one step closer to acting on the thoughts of self-harm, and that scared me more than anything.

I thought the scene in the shower was a one-time thing, but later, as I walked down the hallway to my office, I envisioned myself smashing the picture frame on the wall, picking up a shard of broken glass, and carving my arms. Images of blood smeared all over my clothes and body. It was not a serious contemplation of suicide, but rather a radical desire to cause intense pain to myself in order to make the emotional turmoil stop.

Instead, I buried myself in my work. My only way to survive.

Therapy (Part 1)

January 2014

By the time my therapy appointment arrived, the thoughts of self-harm had dissipated, and I hadn't experienced any more hallucinations. I walked into Rachel's office—a room on the lower level of the bi-level house that served as my one-stop shop for mental health care—and I took a seat on the couch. Rachel was only a few years older than I was, and everything about her appearance was carefully done. Blonde hair neatly pulled back, a white silk shirt below a black blazer, and shoes that had been chosen with purpose. She had an unusual attention to detail with things I was generally oblivious to. I considered her the "self-care pusher," forever suggesting I take myself to the spa or invest in some essential oils or something to that effect. I always laughed at her suggestions; I never took joy in those things, as they made me feel exposed in some way to danger.

She regularly referred to herself as "Dr. Rachel," but it was not long before I dropped the honorific and just called her "Rachel." I could see why she emphasized her doctorate degree. She was clearly proud of her accomplishment, and her degree gave her the ability to offer diagnoses in a way that a person with a master's degree could not. More importantly, though, I knew how necessary it was for a therapist to set boundaries with her clients. As a professor who had to build the same artificial walls between myself and my students, I knew and respected the power differential that existed between Rachel and me. Still, I insisted I was different than the teens she usually saw. To me, she would always be just "Rachel."

I took a seat on the couch while Rachel pushed the door closed and sat on her office chair, which was elevated higher than the couch.

"What's going on?" she asked.

A tear slipped from the corner of my eye straight away. I never liked to cry, but I especially hated to cry in therapy because it made me feel childish. After all, I was a highly respected academic, a person of authority. Although it was part of her job to listen to people talk about their problems, Rachel was a complete stranger to me. I found it pathetic I could not keep it together in front of her, not even for fifteen minutes.

"I don't know. I mean, I saw Dr. Park on Saturday, and she prescribed an antipsychotic medication called Geodon. It made me sick as hell, but I stuck with it because Dr. Park said the side effects would go away. After a few days, I started to feel good, like better than I've felt in a long time. I thought the medication was helping, but in retrospect, I think it was just the mania."

Rachel nodded.

"Then, I became super silly. Susan had to take me to the pharmacy Monday evening. They gave me someone else's antidepressant. Like, they put it under my name and everything. Of course, I didn't take it because I knew it wasn't for me, but what if I had? How dangerous—"

"Unfortunately, pharmacies do make mistakes," she said.

"So we were driving to the pharmacy—it was dark outside—and in the shadows I saw a demon. It zigzagged in the sky and then disappeared." The image in my head was clear. Despite being euphoric at the time, the demon terrified me in the days that followed.

Without flinching, Rachel asked, "Can you describe the demon?"

"It had horns on its head and the body of a praying mantis. I could only see a silhouette because it was dark, but I can draw it for you if you have a piece of paper."

"Please do." She rummaged through her desk and then handed me a sheet of paper and a pen.

In a few seconds, I sketched the demon and handed the paper to Rachel.

"Oh wow," she said. "I can imagine how scary that must have been."

"Well, it was weird because I didn't think it was scary at all. In fact, I became even sillier." The tears flowed more steadily as we got to the core of what was bothering me. Rachel handed me a box of tissues. I took one and blew my nose. "But it's scary, like *really fucking scary*. I mean, look at it—"

Rachel looked down at the paper again. "You are right. I would be scared too. Did you tell Susan?"

Despite having a family history that included serious mental illness, Susan was clueless when it came to the more severe aspects of my bipolar disorder, and the stigma was very real in her reactions and her language. I was terrified of the hallucination, and while I did tell Susan about it the next day, she never brought it up again. When I stared off into the distance, silent and unresponsive, over the next few days, Susan would ask, "What's wrong?" as though I should be getting better. Regardless of what was plaguing my thinking, I would blankly say, "Nothing." Susan would consider it a lie, but I saw it as the truth. *Nothing* was wrong, which is why it made no sense that I had seen the creature in the shadows.

"I told Susan about it the next day. I drew it for her on a piece of paper like I did for you. She said it was creepy, but I don't think she really gets it." I brought my hand to my forehead in exasperation.

Rachel leaned back slightly in her chair. "And what happened after you saw the demon?"

I explained how my good mood didn't last, that, on Tuesday, my skin was crawling and I had thoughts of cutting myself with the razor. I told about how I saw the blood in the shower and how, later, I wanted to smash in the picture frames at work and cut myself.

"I've heard that one before, about smashing picture frames," she said. I could see her wheels turning in thought. "What did you do?"

"Of course, I just kept walking. I mean, I wasn't actually going to smash picture frames at work. I went to my office, I pulled out my laptop, and I worked." I pounded my fist gently on the arm of the couch to emphasize my resolve to work. "It was all I could do to keep the thoughts from entering my head.

It's not like I actually want to die; these visions just enter my head. I had other visions too. Later that day, I was walking to grab lunch and I entered a stairwell. I had a vision of my body being tossed down the stairs. Of course, I'm not going to jump down two flights of stairs, but the image was really scary. Plus, I'm worried that I might accidentally act. I know the statistics of suicide and bipolar—"

I glanced up to see Rachel's reaction. Her brow was furrowed, and her usually cheerful face had turned somber. In an instant, I saw what looked like the formation of a tear in the corner of her eye. I could not be sure though because I was never able to hold eye contact long enough. I quickly looked away.

"This isn't you. It's the illness," she said, firmly but gently. "You know, my friend has bipolar disorder. She attempted suicide last year and had to be hospitalized. She is the sweetest person that you'd ever meet. You'd never think she'd do something like that, but this illness has a way of distorting reality. We've got to keep you safe." She paused and then said, "If it wasn't for your job, I would refer you to in-patient care."

She thinks I should be hospitalized.

The concept of hospitalization made me sick to my stomach. At the time, I believed it was something reserved for the seriously ill, perhaps for those who were damaged beyond repair. While I didn't have in mind the asylums of long ago, I envisioned a sterile floor in the psychiatric wing of a hospital on lockdown, a kind of imprisonment rather than a retreat to safety. I imagined being surrounded by people who were all sicker than me, certainly people who were suicidal or psychotic, but much more dangerous to themselves or others than I was.

No, my illness is not that serious, I maintained.

I brushed the thought aside and assured Rachel I had it under control. After all, I had not acted on any of the thoughts of self-harm, and I was still capable of working despite it all.

"Can you hold out until your appointment with the psychiatrist on Friday?" she asked.

"Yes, I think so."

The wait was agonizing, but two days later I had a follow-up appointment with Dr. Park. Upon hearing about the hallucination and thoughts of self-harm, she changed my antipsychotic medication from Geodon to Zyprexa. After a week on Geodon, she confirmed I was not miraculously cured; I was approaching full-blown mania.

Prelude to the Stranger

January 2014

When people heard that I did my graduate studies at Virginia Tech, the question was always, "Were you there when *it* happened?" *It*, of course, was the mass shooting that took place in 2007. I never knew how to answer this question. Yes, I was a student at the university, but, no, I was not on campus the day the shooting occurred. The shooting took place on a Monday. My classes were held on Tuesdays and Thursdays and, being the hermit I was, I never visited campus unless I absolutely had to. I'm not sure why so many people needed to know the answer to this question. When I responded I wasn't on campus, a voice in the back of my head would whisper, "Yeah, but you *should've* been there."

What many people didn't understand was the shooting in 2007 was only one of a series of unfortunate incidents that occurred at Virginia Tech during that time. Few remembered the manhunt in 2006, in which a prisoner escaped, killing a security guard at the hospital and a police officer near campus. Probably even fewer remember the nightmare in 2009, in which a graduate student decapitated another student in the coffee shop of the Graduate Life Center. I was not on campus for the 2007 shooting. However, I was there the day the escaped prisoner was loose in 2006; I had Susan drive me home from campus after word of a police officer's death reached me. And I wasn't on campus when the murder took place in 2009, but I attended a meeting the following evening in a room right next to the coffee shop. No, I wasn't on campus during the infamous 2007 shooting, but it occurred in the building right next to my home department, a building I had taken classes in, a building I had even lectured in. It was entirely possible that I could've been involved in the shooting. In the nightmares that followed, I *was* a victim.

When a tragedy strikes close to your home, you want to understand what exactly happened. Despite my family's warnings, I spent the days following the shooting glued to the TV watching the story as it unfolded. The tale played over and over until it became my own. It was so easy to place myself in Norris Hall and to reenact the violent scenes reported so graphically in the media; after all, it happened in *my* space. The names and faces of the deceased became etched in my memory. Despite not having known any of them personally, I attended their memorial services and grieved for their loved ones' loss—for my community's loss—until the loss became my own.

Like so many others, the shooting changed me forever. In the months that followed, I was haunted by recurring dreams of a blindingly white classroom stained in blood. I became fearful of classrooms and crowds, obsessively searching for exits and planning my escape in preparation for the inevitable mass murder. Scenarios played out in my head over and over again. It never dawned on me that I had post-traumatic stress disorder, or PTSD, following the shooting. I didn't know an individual doesn't have to directly experience the violence to develop post-traumatic stress symptoms. I suffered immensely from survivor's guilt because I did not feel I was entitled to the nightmares I experienced following the event. *I wasn't in the room*, I kept telling myself. I could not understand why I was plagued with such fear and anxiety. It was not until I started seeking help for bipolar disorder that Rachel also eventually diagnosed me with PTSD. When I looked at the diagnostic criteria, it made complete sense.

Admittedly, over time, things did get easier. I taught a class at Virginia Tech in the year following the shooting, and I finished my classes and defended my dissertation in 2009. Over those two years, I faced my fears and talked myself through incessant irrational thoughts. I counted on the statistics—the likelihood of another mass tragedy striking so close to me was slim. Surely, I had already experienced the worst of what life had to deal me.

In my last semester at Virginia Tech, I entered Norris Hall—the site of the shooting—to obtain a signature required for my graduation. It was the first and only time I had entered the building following the shooting. As I climbed the stairs, I ran my fingers along the cold masonry walls and released some of the tension that I had gripped so tightly over the years. At that moment, it was as if the souls resting in Norris Hall were giving me permission to let go and to move on. I felt like I could finally put it all behind me.

Following the receipt of my doctorate degree, I took a tenure-track position at the University of Michigan. I maintained my fear of classrooms and of public places, but I had become skilled at talking my way through the anxiety. I kept telling myself the chances of it happening again were slim and there was nothing I could do to stop something like that from happening anyway. *You can't live in fear*, I reminded myself. For a time, it worked.

However, in the year leading up to my tenure evaluation, as my moods spiraled out of control, so did my anxiety. The paranoia from the PTSD blended with the paranoia driven by the psychosis. I was on constant alert, the impending doom stalking me wherever I went. As I walked to my office, I became certain there was a sniper on the roof prepared to take out pedestrians. As I faced my class, I was convinced a gunman would burst in at any minute. As I walked down the hallway, I envisioned crowds of people fleeing in terror and heard gunshots in their wake. Over time, the anxiety became even more difficult to manage.

And then a stranger entered my classroom unannounced.

The Stranger

January 2014

It was a brutally cold and windy afternoon. Only sixteen graduate students attended my class in a disproportionately large room, leaving most of the seats empty. I was giving an introductory lecture on energy methods for analyzing the elastic stability of structures, one of my favorite lectures. I had given the students a problem to solve, only to have them discover a solution does not exist if small displacements are assumed. It was one of those lectures that goes absolutely perfectly. At that moment, standing at the head of the classroom, I was totally confident, my timing was spot on, and the students were engaged.

We were two-thirds of the way through the class when the boy—presumably a student from another class—entered the room and slunk into a chair in the front row of the classroom. At first glance, he was no different from any other student, but as I studied him, I was startled by his weasel-like face and menacing eyes. His backpack was heavy as he set it on the floor. He pulled out a notebook and opened it but, unlike the rest of the class, his eyes were trained on me. His face was red as though he were nervous about something. Something about him was off.

A lump formed in my throat as my heart pounded out of my chest.

He has a gun in his backpack. This is it.

My body rattled fiercely with a tremor that crumbled my bones and unleashed powerful waves of terror. I took a deep breath but couldn't stop the violent shaking in my hands and body.

Come on, Ann. Keep it together. Everyone is watching.

I continued to lecture, reciting my lines mechanically while inside, my mind reeled. With all my might, I attempted to steady my hand as I scribbled notes on the chalkboard, but despite my best attempt, the lines came out jagged, my writing barely legible. I put the chalk down.

I turned to the class and attempted to describe concepts I suddenly realized were ridiculously complex and ever so unimportant. As I spoke, he pretended to study the notebook laid out before him, but I kept catching his eye. It was like he was waiting for something. The right moment.

My heart beat faster as the floor shifted under my feet. The room was silent aside from the thumping coming from beneath my sternum. As the blood rushed to my head, I felt my face become flush.

It's only twelve degrees outside, I mustered as I tried to give a reason for his red face.

I pretended like everything was normal and posed questions to the class with a nervous smile. Each syllable was uttered with care in an attempt to convey a sense of normalcy. All the while, he and I kept our eyes locked on each other.

He will take me out first. Yes, I will be the first to go.

I frantically searched the room for a way out. No windows. The room was wider than it was long, with a door at either side. I stood on a stage in the front of the room. He was in a section to the left. I could run to the exit on the right, but he would get me before I reached the door. I was too obvious of a target. Even if I got out of the classroom, it would be easy for him to catch me down the hallway. I could step across the hallway to my office, but the door was locked. I would fumble with my keys. I could run to one of my colleagues' offices down the hall, close the door behind me, and jump from the window. It was only fifteen feet at most to the ground.

But what about my students? I can't leave them behind.

As the second hand clicked one beat forward, I felt the moment draw nearer. My words were coming out awkward and wrong. I was losing control. Fight or flight. *Run. Should I run?* Heat rushed over my body, the sickening and dizzying feeling that preceded the blackness of fainting. The sound of my voice became muffled as though I was talking under water. I was drowning. Flailing to maintain consciousness, following distorted light at the surface that signified life. In my desperation, I made a last-ditch attempt to save myself.

Don't let him make the first move. Don't...

"Okay, uh, I'm looking at my notes, and it doesn't make sense for us to start something new," I muddled. "Let's go ahead and stop here for today." I scrambled to collect my notes and raced for the door.

In the hallway, the keys jingled in my hands as I tried to fit the right key into the lock of my office door. I turned the key, pushed the door open, and then slammed it behind me, making sure it was locked. My attempts to rationalize what had happened were futile; the panic had already taken over. There was nothing left to do except move to a safe place until the episode passed. "I need to get out of here," I cried under my breath. As quickly as I could, I threw on my coat and hat, grabbed my backpack, and hurried to the nearest exit.

The wind stung me with a sharpness that could only come with reality. It was a harsh reminder that what had happened was indeed real and that, yes, I was truly in the midst of losing my mind. I walked at a pace that was practically a jog, trying to hold back the tears until I reached the safety of my van. Once inside, I began hyperventilating. Piercing inhale. Shallow exhale. The tears cascaded down my face as I heaved in gasps for air. I attempted to steady myself and slow my breathing, but it was useless.

"Why?!" I screamed as I pounded the steering wheel. "Why is this happening?!"

It was not just a question as to why the stranger had entered my classroom. It was a question of why *all* of it was happening—the moods, the demon, the voices, the suicidal thoughts, and now the realization of my most horrific nightmare.

The panic lasted for only a few minutes and was followed by an odd feeling of relief—relief I had *survived*, as if I had narrowly escaped tragedy. I had had paranoia over school shootings before, but this was the first time I believed I was in imminent danger. I had failed reasoning through it this time. I could not tell what was real. I could not tell if I was safe.

The only thing I knew was I needed to do something quickly. I dialed Rachel's number and left her a panicked voicemail. Rachel, of course, knew about my fear of school shootings. She knew my tragic history at Virginia Tech and would be able to decipher the meaning behind my message. She responded quickly and fit me into her schedule the following day.

In the evening, I came home to Susan, who immediately walked up to me and wrapped her arms gently around me.

"How are you?" she asked with a look of genuine concern.

"Terrible," I said. At her suggestion, I had taken the afternoon off from work and stopped by a coffee shop for a restorative pot of green tea. I felt mildly better after pouring my emotions into the journal I kept on me. However, the calmness that came with the self-care did not last.

"I'm so sorry this happened."

"I know. I just—" I could not find the words to express the sensations I felt.

"Go and have a seat in the living room. I'll fix dinner."

I lay on the couch, staring at the darkness outside the window, my mind consumed by the events that had unfolded earlier in the day. Skye busied herself with building a house for Kipper, our cat, out of blankets and pillows. She was so engrossed in the activity she did not ask for my involvement. Before Skye was born, Susan and I worried about the kind of world we might bring a child into. While dangers always existed regardless of generation, the threats of school shootings had become all too common in today's world. Skye was too little to understand any of it, but no doubt she would be programmed in the world of active shooter drills; it was only a matter of time. I had always hoped Skye would be an agent for change when she grew up, a voice of compassion and a leader with empathy. She certainly showed signs of compassion and kindness towards her peers, and she didn't fear taking on challenges. Maybe she would be part of the solution someday. Maybe. But for now, I was tangled in my own web of emotions from today's close call.

Dinner followed shortly and, despite my lack of appetite, I managed to eat the plate of vegetable stir-fry sitting in front of me. I was mostly silent as Susan moved on to talking about her day at work. Unlike my day, hers was nothing more than ordinary. I tried to listen with feigned interest, but I simply could not focus. My mind began to wander back to the classroom.

"What's wrong?" she finally asked after realizing I was not paying attention to anything she was saying.

"I'm sorry. I'm just so bothered by what happened today. I mean, why would someone enter a room in the middle of class like that?"

"He was just a student. Probably a student from the next class." Seeing that I was not buying her explanation, she followed with, "You have nothing to worry about."

Nothing to worry about. It was the same response I had given her a hundred times before, the times when she would spring from bed in the middle of the night and peer through the curtains looking for the intruder lurking in the shadows. I would roll over and fall back to sleep while she gripped the baseball bat she kept by the bedside, ready to attack. I tried to be understanding, but her fears were silly and exhausting.

After all, there was *nothing* to worry about.

"I know. But I'm terrified he is going to come back," I said. I drew my hands into fists, not to hit anyone or anything but to hold on to *something*. I was beginning to get frustrated she could not follow my reasoning that the intruder was most definitely going to kill me.

"And so what? He is just a student. What is he going to do? *Study?*" she said sarcastically.

I shook my head. "I don't think I can teach again."

"What are you talking about? You are *fine*," she insisted. She began gathering the plates from the table, clanking the dishes in clear irritation with me.

Our voices were escalating to the tone of an argument. There were times when I might have started yelling at this point in the conversation, calling Susan cruel and criticizing her for her lack of understanding. But this time, I was not looking for a fight, so I backed down. I knew her logic was sounder than mine. However, her telling me not to worry was pointless and, in fact, a little demoralizing. I wanted her to say my fears were justified, that it was probably best if I gave up on teaching altogether for my safety and the safety of my students because, after all, I would be the one at fault if a shooting took place in my classroom. It was my job to keep my students safe, and what better way to keep them safe than to cancel class for eternity?

"Okay. You're right," I said evenly. I didn't believe it, but I wasn't getting anywhere with her. I took Skye to bed. I mentioned nothing more to Susan about the classroom incident even though it was all I could think about.

That night was dreadfully long and filled with a horror so intense it knocked the dust from my age-old nightmares. In the blackness of my mind, I stood before the class. The same dark room I had taught in since I first became a professor. He paced outside of the doorway, hesitated, and then entered the room. We made eye contact. I froze. He reached into a backpack, discarded on the floor, and pulled a semi-automatic handgun. Boom-boom-boom. Bodies, screams, blood. I frantically searched for a way out. Nowhere to run, nowhere to hide. He looked at me, caught my eyes like the boy in the class had. No words, but I knew he had been searching just for me. He aimed his gun. One final boom. In searing pain, I fell to the floor. Warm, sticky blood trickled out, red and wet, puddling around me. The scene faded to black. And started again.

Therapy (Part 2)

January 2014

Rachel walked me down to her office and guided me to sit on the couch. The space was dimly lit, making the room seem almost cavernous. A lamp stood in the corner, emitting yellow light, while pale blue sunlight crept in through the window just above ground level. My mind was hazy with the lack of sleep and the tears that had fallen through the night.

"So tell me, what's going on?"

What's going on?

It was merely a formality, a way to get the conversation started. We both knew why I was there. An unsettling calmness drifted over me. A calm that follows a raging storm, the moment when observers stand there stunned and wondering if what had happened was real and whether more danger lay ahead.

The only thing I could do was relay the facts.

"I was teaching yesterday when a stranger came into my classroom. He sat in the front row and pulled out his notebook like he was studying or something. But in my mind, he had a gun and was planning to shoot up my class. I ended class abruptly, and then I ran to my car and had a panic attack."

"Was he real?"

"I...I don't know." Crushed by the weight of the question, I felt a tear break through and roll gently down my cheek, leaving its cold, wet trail behind. I had not considered perhaps the stranger was not real. The psychosis had been certainly bad at the time. I had been suffering from severe paranoia, and just a few days earlier I had seen the demon and battled the flood of suicidal thoughts. I could not trust myself anymore.

I crossed my right leg over my left in a figure four and hugged it toward me, trying to maintain control over what I could. "Whether he's real or not, I don't think I will be able to teach tomorrow."

"Okay, well, what can you do in class tomorrow to make you feel safer? Could you lock the door to your classroom?" she suggested.

Locking classroom doors was a touchy subject. The investigation following the Virginia Tech shooting found the shooter was able to enter the classrooms easily because none of the doors in Norris Hall had locks. The university made several upgrades to the buildings on campus in the year following the shooting, including the installation of locks on every single classroom door on campus. Other universities had not followed suit. I had inspected the handles on the classroom doors on North Campus and found the doors did not lock from the inside. If a shooter tried to enter my classroom, I was absolutely powerless.

"The doors don't have locks," I said.

"Could you at least shut the door to your classroom?"

"Yeah," I said, realizing it would not do anything to stop a shooter from entering my classroom. It might keep a student from rudely interrupting my class though. I tapped my foot swiftly. "What do I do about the anxiety? I am still convinced someone is going to shoot up my class. I know it's irrational, but I can't seem to shake the thought."

Rachel paused for a moment. I was pretty sure I was the only client of hers who had lived through a school shooting. Even though Virginia Tech was a large public university, it must have been a rarity to meet someone who had been a student there when it happened. I suspected therapists were armed with all kinds of tools to help individuals with PTSD, but I did not realize at the time that school shootings were a kind of uncharted territory. The tragedy at Virginia Tech had touched the nation, and many people who had no affiliation with the university were severely affected by the event. I can only imagine how difficult it must have been for Rachel to guide me through, but I did not sense her uneasiness with the subject until later on.

"I think in your situation, much of the anxiety has to do with the fact you feel powerless. Each time you relive the event, you are a helpless victim. There is an exercise I do with some of my clients who have PTSD that I think might help you. What we need to do is change the story so you are no longer powerless."

I took a moment to weigh my options. I was fervently opposed to therapy exercises that involved any sort of active exploration of my thoughts. Mind-bending exercises that prodded my subconscious were not things to play around with. Done poorly, they could do more harm than good.

However, I desperately needed help. I had to trust Rachel knew what she was doing. She was the expert and, while I did not like to admit it, she had done a pretty good job up to that point.

After my initial hesitation, I agreed and followed Rachel's lead.

"I want you to imagine you are in the classroom," she began slowly, her voice soft. "The attacker is there. The more detail you can give the scene, the better. Go ahead and describe what you see."

I closed my eyes and allowed my imagination to wander. "I'm in the classroom that I normally teach in. There's a small stage at the front of the room where I stand. The room has tables and chairs where the students sit."

"And where is the attacker?"

"He comes in through the door on the left and sits down. His backpack is heavy. I hear it as he sets it on the floor." The familiar scene played forward, causing my palms to sweat.

"Good. And what happens next?"

I swallowed. "He pulls a gun from his backpack and starts shooting."

"Okay, now what we are going to do is change the ending. You are no longer powerless. What if you had a gun of your own and shot him first?" Rachel asked.

"No, I'm afraid of guns."

"What about a knife, and you stab him before he gets a shot off?" she suggested.

"No, I don't like knives."

"What then?" she prompted.

I thought for a moment, my heart still trying to climb its way into my throat. "A chair. I could be standing by with a chair and throw it at him."

"Yes! Perfect."

There was something about pretending to be powerful that actually made me feel powerful. It was similar to the techniques I used when I became anxious before giving a presentation or having to talk to strangers at a social function. I would plant my feet in the ground, stand tall, and pretend that I was someone with confidence and poise. After faking it for so long, I eventually became that person. Even though I had been doubtful Rachel's little exercise would work, my heartbeat slowed, my breathing steadied, and my fists were clenched in power. *I would fight.*

After working through the scene, Rachel asked how I felt.

"Better," I said, somewhat amazed at the sense of relief.

"So what are you going to do tomorrow?"

"I'm going to close the doors at the start of class."

"And if you see him again?"

I hesitated and then rehearsed, "I will confront him."

"Right. You can do this," she said.

The next day, I sat in my office, watching the minute hand tick forward until it was time for class. My pulse doubled as I collected my notebook and opened my office door. I closed my eyes. *If you close the door to your classroom, he most likely will not enter. If he enters the room, you will confront him after class; he is just a kid with poor manners. If he is going to start shooting, there is nothing you can do to stop him.*

Despite the power I felt in Rachel's office, I still did not feel secure standing in front of the class. But I planted my feet and spoke with authority, running images through my mind of me throwing a chair at the intruder as I taught. I found what had started as false assurance turned into genuine confidence with time. After practicing the scene over and over, I had a lot more courage to charge at the mythical gunman who was going to enter my classroom. I would attack *him*, rather than flee in fear or yield submissively. We reached the end of class, and to my surprise, no one entered my classroom unexpectedly. After class, I gathered my notes and stood in the hallway with chalk dust on my hands, watching as students poured into the room. I looked intently at everyone who entered to see if I might see him again, but he did not appear. Whether he was real or not, I was relieved.

Med Check

January 2014

I sat in the waiting room, watching bursts of air swirl the snow past the front window. There weren't many cars in the parking lot, and there was no one else in the waiting room. It was silent except for the white noise machines sitting on the floor at either end of the room. A small whiteboard sat in the entrance with room assignments for the doctors and therapists who were in the building that day. Dr. Park was in Room 4, which I assumed was the tiny room on the main level that we normally met in. Dr. Rachel was downstairs in Room 1, and I desperately hoped she and I did not cross paths. While I was establishing a trust in her, I had no desire to see her outside of our normal meeting time. Impromptu encounters—even at her place of work—made me anxious because Rachel reminded me of the ugly side of me that showed every time I talked to her. I checked the clock overhead to make sure she would be in session with someone other than me, and then I pulled out my journal in an attempt to prepare for my appointment.

After a moment, a woman with a small child rushed into the building. I gave a smile to the little girl, who must have been close in age to Skye, and then glanced at the mother, who paid no attention to me. The woman was like most of the people I had seen in the waiting room—there was nothing extraordinary about her. She was merely a woman who was lugging her daughter around to a doctor's appointment on a blustery Saturday morning.

I nodded my head and then turned my eyes to my journal.

Dr. Park had been tweaking my medications, and I was becoming frustrated I still was not better. My moods cycled, and I still had symptoms of psychosis. I had a feeling another change in medication lay ahead. I assembled a list of items I needed to report to the doctor on the first blank page I could find in my journal. In black ink, I wrote, "Not sleeping well. Panic over student entering classroom. Anxious about teaching. Irritable. More upbeat than usual. Heard static." I paused for a moment, questioning whether I should disclose my most recent hallucination to Dr. Park, and then I jotted down, "Woman whispered 'murder' in my ear." I couldn't bear reading those last few words.

I should have known I was cycling back into mania because ordinary details like a rising sun peering through curtains were suddenly spectacular. Just the other morning, as I relished in the splendor of the light illuminating my bedroom, a woman had leaned close to me and slowly uttered "mur-der." Not as a command but rather as an observation. Her voice was the same clean voice that regularly whispered my name close to my ear, the voice that caused me to start and look frantically around, finding myself alone on so many occasions. It was unusual for me to hear her say anything other than my name, never mind a word so violent. While she was not commanding me to harm anyone, I was sickened. Were things getting worse? Would the doctor want to hospitalize me? At what moment would I become an actual danger to my family or others?

"Ann?" I jumped when Dr. Park greeted me from the other side of the waiting room. I quickly closed my journal and followed her back to her office.

"How are you doing?" she asked as I took a seat.

"I'm okay," I lied, and then I corrected myself. "I mean, I had this really weird situation where a stranger entered my class and sat down. I'm not sure what he was doing there, but I was convinced he had a gun and was going to start shooting."

"What did you do?"

"I was about to have a panic attack, so I ended class early and left campus."

"Was he real?"

I took a deep breath. Despite confirming with one of my students that a stranger did in fact enter the classroom, I could not help thinking my mind had made the whole situation up. I had no clue what my psychosis was capable of, and it seemed plausible my mind was playing off my fear of school shootings.

"I think so," I replied. Then I corrected myself. "I mean, yes. I'm pretty sure he was real."

She looked at me skeptically and then wrote something down in my chart. My heart flitted into my throat.

I followed up by saying, "I've been working on the anxiety with Rachel in therapy."

"Good," she said without looking up, as she continued to write.

I made my way down the list, describing my lack of sleep, my extreme irritability, and my increased level of activity. My mouth was becoming dry from talking. I swallowed hard, hoping my tongue would not trip on the next few words. "I've been hearing static and, uh—how do I say this?" She looked up from her notes, and, as though I was pulling off a Band-Aid, I blurted, "I heard a woman whisper 'murder.'" Dr. Park's eyes widened a little, and then, fearing she was going to send me straight to the hospital, I downplayed the situation. "I mean, she just uttered the word; it's not like she was telling me to act on it. It was just a little scary."

"I'll bet," she said. "And have you had any other symptoms of psychosis?"

"I've heard other whispering. Most of the time, I can't tell what the voice is saying. Other times, I have heard my name but nothing else."

After listening carefully, Dr. Park planned a course of action. The evidence was clear: I was experiencing symptoms of mania and having auditory hallucinations. The standard course of action was to adjust my medications.

"Let's keep the Lamictal the same and increase the Zyprexa," she concluded.

I was leery about increasing the antipsychotic medication because I was already experiencing side effects, most notably weight gain. In fact, in a period of a few weeks, I had put on nearly ten pounds. I noticed it mostly in my pants. My jeans had become unbearably tight. I squeezed them over my thighs each morning and tugged the waist closed, wondering how much longer it would be before the button would give.

My swollen belly often spilled out over the top, and I found my choices in shirts rather limited—I needed a shirt that was baggy enough to hide the bulge that had appeared around my waist. As the days went on, I was constantly reminded by my discomfort that, to put it bluntly, I was getting fat.

I had never really been conscious about my figure because I had maintained nearly the same weight my entire adult life. On the Zyprexa though, my appetite had nearly doubled. I would eat my lunch only to find my stomach empty an hour later. I could not tolerate the hunger pains, so I would walk to the coffee shop in the student center. My mind told me to get something light and healthy, but my body craved the most fattening, sugary option it could find. When I reached the counter, I would request a pastry from the glass case and, like an addict getting her fix, I would find the nearest table, unwrap the goods, and wait for the sweetness to flood my veins. As soon as the last bite was gone, I was left with a craving for more, a feeling I was forced to dismiss. I would walk back to my office feeling guilty and ashamed by my lack of self-control and hoping no one I knew saw me gorging on pastries every day.

"Okay," I said reluctantly, without mentioning my concern about weight gain. Instead, I made a silent promise to myself to be more disciplined about my eating habits and considered it was possibly time to start visiting the gym again.

I walked out of Dr. Park's office and into the cold parking lot. My shoulders relaxed and breathing became easier. She did not make a big deal out of the voice; she didn't even suggest hospitalization. I looked at the prescription slip, which indicated the increase in Zyprexa, and scowled, but I put it in my pocket, resolved to get the prescription filled nonetheless. I tried to be optimistic. Perhaps it would stop the psychosis. Perhaps my weight gain would eventually taper off. Perhaps I would not feel dizzy or nauseated or exhausted all the time. Perhaps.

Plowing the Driveway

February 2014

The wind ripped across the plains like fingernails on a chalkboard, tossing heaps of snow in the roadways with each piercing shriek. The ghostly howls seemed unearthly, as though the demons that haunted me were the only ones who could inhabit that godforsaken plot of land Susan and I owned. Each gust of wind blasted my face with a dusting of snow that quickly melted against my warmth, leaving my face wet and cold. The rest of my body was safely protected in my winter gear—the layers of fleece and flannel tucked beneath my impenetrable coat and snow pants, the woolen scarf wrapped tightly around my chin, and my trusted leather mittens that had carried me through several snowboarding seasons in southwestern Pennsylvania.

I trod through the snow to get to the barn, where the plow truck was stored.

My god, how much snow has fallen?

My boot prints measured eight—maybe ten—inches of snowfall. The tracks from my last run down the driveway with the plow were no longer visible.

I'll never make it down the driveway in this mess.

I bit my bottom lip beneath the scarf and closed my eyes.

Truth be told, I didn't have a choice. If I couldn't clear a path, we would have no hope of getting out at all. I had set my alarm for four o'clock so I could clear the driveway before leaving for work. However, I had completely underestimated the snowfall and obviously had not considered the drifts that had piled up like Saharan sand dunes. Their geometric complexities were both mesmerizing and terrifying. The snow blew around the drifts like a mystical fog as the piles morphed and grew right before my eyes. Around the edges of the pole barn, the drifts easily reached two feet in depth.

My heart stuttered, but I attempted to suppress the feeling of panic, even as I pictured the plow truck slamming into the icy depths.

Slipping off my right mitten, I unlocked the rotted barn door with a bare hand and stepped inside quickly, feeling up and down the wall for the light switch. The halogen light hummed and flickered then brightened as it warmed up. The red pick-up stared me down with its makeshift plow that Susan's mom had bought online for a thousand bucks. The hunk of bent and welded metal had been assembled by a high school shop teacher in Ohio. The first time I used the plow, one of the welds fractured, and the man had to bring a replacement plow. It was built with good intentions, but in all honesty, the plow was a piece of junk—and all we could afford.

I pushed the button to raise the oversized garage door, climbed into the Ford, and fired up the engine. I knew half a foot of snow was about all the measly plow could handle. Nonetheless, I lowered it to the ground using a remote-controlled winch and pushed out of the barn. I burst through the snowdrift that barricaded the barn and then prayed the truck maintained its course the rest of the way down the driveway.

"Come on, come on," I said under my breath as the truck skated across the freshly fallen snow. There were no markings to indicate where the driveway was, so I had to rely on memory. I used the trees to gauge vague distance. The land was flat and the driveway straight for the most part, so it was not critical I stay on the path.

About fifteen yards in, the truck stopped. I gave it more gas, and the wheels spun out.

"Shit!" I yelled and beat my mittened hands on the steering wheel.

I jumped out and grabbed the shovel from the bed of the truck. Snow and gravel had piled up in front of the plow, and skid marks had formed under the tires. I stabbed the shovel into the snow and heaved it, bit by bit, away from the plow.

Once the snow blockage was cleared, I threw the shovel into the bed of the truck, climbed back inside, raised the plow with the remote-controlled winch, and reversed a few feet. I lowered the plow, straightened the wheel, and gassed it. The truck trundled forward. A few more yards, and then—*thud*—stuck again. I slammed the gear shift into park, jumped out, shoveled furiously, and then climbed back in and proceeded on my way.

I continued working that way for a good hour. Each time I was stuck, I grew even more furious and frantic, shouting obscenities while I held back the tears that were freezing in the corners of my eyes. Eventually, I became careless, slamming down on the gas pedal as the truck fishtailed to a raging halt. After letting out a disturbing laugh—the kind a supervillain might give—I pounded the snow erratically with the shovel, and then, with my fists, shouting threats at the storm in a way that would have made little sense to an observer. I was clearly fighting a battle of good versus evil, but no outsider would be able to tell which side I was on and, regardless, I was sorely losing. To make matters worse, the wind was growing stronger, which made me ill with the fear we could lose power and—because the house was on a well—water, too.

No food. No heat. No water. No way out.

"We have to get out of here," I said through gritted teeth. Failure was not an option this time.

About halfway down the thousand-foot driveway, the truck thudded to a halt once again. Once again, I began shoveling the snow away from the plow when the wind let out a shriek. Above me and the truck, the limbs of the pines waved violently against the violet sky. The hair stood up on the back of my neck. *Someone is watching me.*

I glanced in all directions, not exactly sure of what to expect. I looked up to see a figure in the window of the neighbor's house. It was a large man with broad shoulders, a man I had neither seen nor met before.

A rapist. A filthy rapist. The kind of man who kidnaps women and locks them in a basement. He's watching me. That sick bastard.

I quickly looked away. I felt like I was either going to pass out or throw up. Beneath my winter gear, I had been sweating. I unzipped my coat to cool my body. The wind chill was below zero, and yet I was overheating.

I took a deep breath and closed my eyes. "This isn't real," I whispered to myself. "There is no man in the house."

It was quite possible there was a man in the house. After all, people did live in the house, and there was a light on in the bedroom where I saw the figure. However, I knew it was highly unlikely a man would be watching me, especially with some sort of twisted intent of kidnapping me in the midst of this snowstorm at four o'clock in the morning. It didn't make sense. I forced myself to look again at the figure. I studied him closely, to see if I had seen him before and to identify what it was about him that terrified me. When I looked up though, all I saw was a shadow caused by an open closet door.

I looked away and then looked back. At first glance, the shadow did look like a broad-shouldered man, but a close inspection revealed it was only the outline of the closet door. My eyes—and mind—were playing tricks on me.

Still, I seemed to prefer the false reality. Part of me *wanted* to be in danger. I kept looking at the house, hoping to see the man, certain he was going to take me hostage. When I finally accepted it was a door's shadow, my mind drifted into other distortions.

Perhaps there are demons lurking in the shadows, preparing to carry me off to some hell-like world, I thought, as I sensed the presence of creatures in trees nearby. I jumped at the rustling of branches.

Back to shoveling. *Hurry.*

I began shoveling as quickly as I could, not out of anger but rather out of fear of what would happen to me—or what *was* happening to me—as I fought the snow in the darkness of the early morning. When I realized my mind was venturing into such dark territory, I knew I needed to finish the plow job and get back to the safety of my home.

It was not long before I reached the end of the driveway. I did a three-point turn in the middle of the empty dirt road and pulled back into the driveway with my eyes set on the barn. As I drove toward it, I kept the plow to the ground in an attempt to widen the tracks down the driveway, but the truck instead swerved back and forth, knocking heaps of snow back into the middle of the path I had just cleared. Without hesitation, I drove on and merely shook my head. In the barn, I threw the gearshift into park. I gripped the steering wheel until my hands burned, still holding back those frozen tears.

Failing You

March 2014

I lay on the couch, immobile, taking in the weight of all that had happened in the past few weeks. Life had become so heavy, with the persistent hallucinations, the mood swings, and the impending threat of danger on campus.

Skye played on the floor with her Duplo blocks. Her little hands stacked red, yellow, green, and blue blocks into a tower that nearly dwarfed her. Toys were strewn all over the living room, the telltale signs a small child inhabited our home. Skye was my child but not by birth. We conceived Skye by artificial insemination, or IUI, with sperm from an anonymous donor. Before Skye was born, I fixated on the fact that I would not be biologically related to her. I recall digging through donor profiles, which could be sorted by race, hair color, area of academic study, and more, to find the magical one that matched me exactly. I was nearly in tears as I tried to determine if I was more of a Ben Affleck or a Fred Savage. In the end, I must have picked the right donor because Susan got pregnant on the first attempt, and the child who was born from her womb was perfect in every way. I thought not being biologically related to Skye would make me somehow inferior to Susan, but I learned something incredibly important the day Skye was born: biology doesn't make a family; love makes a family.

Parenting in a same-sex household was much like any other household, but there were certain things that had to be figured out along the way. I discovered it didn't matter what she called us, and there was no real disadvantage to not having a man in the house. We got all sorts of questions and comments making us think those things were important, but the fact of the matter was that Skye would find *someone* to take her to the Daddy-Daughter Dance. The real struggle we faced was the insecurity we lived with that, because same-sex parents could not *both* be granted parental rights to a child in the state of Michigan, I had no legal rights to her. It wasn't until two years after she was born that I adopted Skye in sheer secrecy, taking advantage of a loophole in the adoption laws in South Carolina. My name was finally on her birth certificate, and I had the court order to back it up.

I stared out the picture window at the trees in our front yard. My eyes played games, making shapes in the bare branches of the trees. Faces, right angles, patterns. It was as if I was searching for something but always coming up short. Susan set a basket of laundry next to the couch, grabbed a glass of water, and sat down on the loveseat.

"What's wrong?" she asked.

Without looking away from the picture window, I answered, "Nothing."

"You look like you are about to cry."

"Oh," I said, surprised she was able to pick up on my mood

so easily. "I'm just sad."

"Do you want to talk about it?"

"I don't know."

"Ann?" Susan could always tell when I was lying.

Skye continued to play with her blocks, making a vehicle out of a block connected to two sets of wheels and using it to drive a person around the newly constructed block tower. She paid no attention to our conversation.

After a moment, I looked to Susan and said, "I feel like I am failing you."

"What do you mean?" she asked.

I paused. "I mean, it's all my fault that we are in this whole mess. It's just, I really wanted to get pregnant. I tried so hard. Eight IUIs, that horrible polypectomy—I tried *so hard* for Skye to have a sibling." Tears streamed from my eyes. "Now we have to deal with the bipolar, the psychosis..." My voice trailed off.

"There's nothing you could do about it." Susan sat next to me on the couch and wrapped her arm around me.

Skye was getting older, and I worried if Susan and I waited too long, the gap in age between Skye and our second child would be too great that the two would not bond closely in the way siblings should. I felt like I was a failure for having to give up on trying to conceive, but at the same time, part of me was relieved it was over. Fertility treatments were dreadful, and the whole process left me hating the fact I was ever born a woman. I was sick of monitoring my cycles and taking the fertility medications and lying on a cold table in a hospital gown with my feet in stirrups, hoping this time the insemination would take.

As I cried softly, Skye jumped up and said, "Watch this Mama!" She pushed the tower to the ground and blocks flew everywhere.

"Whoa! Good job, kiddo. Can you build an even bigger tower?" I said, wiping the tears from my eyes. I sniffled hard. I was trying to play the part of a good mom, but everything about me was off.

Susan lay against me and gave me a hug. I heard her sniffle.

"It's okay," she said. "Everything is going to be okay."

I let her hold me for a minute, and then I sat up and lay my head on her shoulder.

"And you haven't failed me," she said. She bent her head down to make eye contact with me, but I held my head against her shoulder. She was the only thing holding me to earth.

"But we didn't get pregnant, and I don't think I can try anymore. You know, I thought the fertility clinic was out to get me, don't you?"

"What?" Susan asked, caught completely off-guard.

"I don't know when it started exactly, but I remember sitting on the table at the last IUI. Remember, I was left waiting for over an hour in my hospital gown before they did the procedure?"

Susan nodded.

"I couldn't help thinking about the donor specimen. Did they thaw it at the time of my appointment, or did they wait an hour until they were ready to do the procedure? It makes a difference doesn't it?"

"Sure."

"Well, I heard chatter coming in from the air vent. Two nurses were joking and laughing and carrying on. I couldn't help but think they were joking and laughing *about me*, that they were secretly trying to sabotage our IUI specimen. They were carrying on about how I wasn't going to get pregnant yet again. I mean, they are a fertility clinic: they make more money if you *don't* get pregnant, right? Well, I almost got off of that table and ran out the door, but the nurse came in."

"Were they really talking and laughing, or were you hearing things?" Susan crooked her neck so she could see my eyes. Her gaze was backed with genuine concern.

"I don't know. Part of me thinks it was the psychosis. I mean, I am sick. I was unwell when we were trying to get pregnant. I never trusted that doctor, but I also don't trust myself right now. Either way, it freaked me out."

"Let's not worry about it. No more getting pregnant for now." She reached her hand out to pat my forearm.

"I'm afraid this bipolar thing is going to be harder to control than I originally thought."

"It's okay. We will get through this," she said. "And we can always try adoption when you're ready."

"You won't feel bad about giving up?" I asked.

"Adoption is not giving up. Plus, you know I've always dreamed of adopting a child. Even if we had a whole bunch of kids on our own, I always thought we would adopt at least one kid." She paused a minute, and then said, "Just focus on yourself right now. You've got a lot going on."

"Yeah," I said. It took me a moment to absorb what she had said. *Just focus on yourself right now.*

"And the stranger who came into my class..."

"You're still worried about that?" Her tone had changed from supportive to one of exhaustion.

I nodded.

"You seriously have nothing to worry about. It was nothing," she insisted.

I sat up straight. "But I can't stop thinking about a shooting every time I have to teach. When I walk down the hallways, I hear gunshots and imagine people fleeing. I'm *terrified*."

"Have you told your therapist?"

I wanted to tell her therapy wasn't working, that it wasn't enough, that things were not getting better, but instead, I said, "Yes, we've been working on it."

"Well, that's good. It'll get better," she said. Then she added with an attempt at enthusiasm, "Plus, the semester is almost over."

"I guess you're right." I paused for a moment in reflection, and then I said, "Thanks. I do feel a little better. After talking, I mean."

"Good," Susan said. I leaned back into the couch, while Susan reached over and started folding one of the towels she had set nearby.

"And you know you can always talk to me, right?" she said.

Without looking her in the eye, I said, "Yeah." I still didn't feel comfortable talking to her about my mental illness. I tried to keep my fears about the stranger to myself because anytime I brought it up, the response was always the same: talk to your therapist about it. The fact was I talked about it every week with Rachel and I still did not feel any better. I shuddered at the thought of how unwell I was, and then I quickly changed the subject.

Pennsylvania Stabbing

April 2014

The winter stretched on, but sometime around March, the days grew longer and the birds started to sing. Spring was supposed to be a time of hope and renewal, but while I possessed a small amount of hope things were going to get better, the truth was I was barely keeping it together. Not only was I certain a school shooting was imminent, I was still battling a flood of mood swings. I was continuously swinging back and forth between mania and depression, although the Lamictal dampened the severity. The psychotic symptoms were still apparent too, though they were minor in comparison to those I'd experienced in January. My hallucinations had become limited to the occasional whispering in my ear or shadow in my peripheral vision. I experienced severe paranoia, but it was hard to tell if it was brought on by the psychosis or by the PTSD. I attended therapy regularly and attempted to work through the anxiety that made my job a living hell. At the same time, I was working with Dr. Park to find a medication cocktail that worked. I counted down the days to the end of the semester when I would be released from my teaching duties for the summer and have the time and energy to recover my health.

Despite all this, I continued to go to work every day. I stood at the front of the classroom and lectured on material I no longer cared about. Each and every time I entered the classroom, I was sure I was putting my life on the line. And while most faculty spent their class time engaging with the students, I kept my head down and avoided eye contact for I feared that, if I took a moment to scan the room, I would find the weasel-faced boy glaring back at me. Thus, I entered the classroom with my eyes to the ground, and I immediately turned my back on the students under the guise of needing to write notes on the board. I did not bother to face the class and see if there were any questions. In fact, there were questions. Hands raised crookedly in the air until, after several minutes, the students realized their attempts to get my attention were futile. The hands silently came down, and the moments were later recorded on end-of-term course evaluations. My scores on teaching evaluations remained higher than the department average, but they were lower than my peak, and the critical comments were new.

One afternoon, I returned to my office from a departmental committee meeting. I pulled my peanut butter sandwich from my backpack, sat down at my desk, and opened my browser. The homepage of my browser was tuned to the national news, and, while I had been routinely triggered by the in-your-face reporting of the mainstream media, I believed it was my obligation—as an educated member of society—to keep up with current events in the U.S. and abroad. Most days, I periodically scanned the headlines for any events I found relevant. It was my way of staying connected with what was going on in the world, just as my parents read the newspaper and watched the evening news each day. Generally, I relished in being informed, but I also knew the shock of some headlines escalated my anxiety to an unnecessary level. Violent things happened in the world, and my creative imagination placed me at the center of some of the most disturbing situations.

I swallowed a bite of my sandwich, and, as the browser popped up, I gasped at the ticker at the top of the page, highlighted in yellow with letters all in caps: "BREAKING NEWS." Of course, I had to click the link. After the Virginia Tech shooting, I was drawn to any headline that involved mass violence in a public space. Upon clicking the link, I saw the unfolding of a stabbing that had occurred at a high school in southwestern Pennsylvania. Because the event had just taken place, there was little information provided by the article, and experience told me the information provided was only partially accurate. The media, as usual, fed the hype as they sought to provide information as quickly as possible. The updates came in by the minute, so I constantly, incessantly refreshed the page for any new information. It was a familiar frenzy, one I had taken on in nearly every instance of mass violence since 2007.

The Pennsylvania incident did not involve anyone I knew. Moreover, the attacker was using knives rather than guns, meaning the number of casualties was surely less than what was the case at Virginia Tech. Nonetheless, as I frantically sought information about the stabbing, I flashed back to the news clips that haunted me from Virginia Tech. Images passed through my mind of police cars circling Tech's campus, ambulances with sirens blaring, and the wounded being carted from the battlefield with electrical cords used as tourniquets. With the Virginia Tech shooting, the newscasters had altered their reports as deaths and injuries were tallied, while investigators had pieced together information about the suspect. Attempts to answer the questions of "who," "why," and "how" had emerged rapidly. Reading about the Pennsylvania stabbing, I was carried back to that fateful day in 2007.

The incident in Pennsylvania struck a chord with me. Yet another tragedy in a school, and this one was so close to my hometown. The stabbing occurred at a high school just minutes from the school where my mom taught. It could have been my mom's school. The thought of it made me ill. It was just one more reminder that none of us is safe, that these things can and do strike close to home, eventually. Most people are capable of handling such devastating news without missing a beat. I know this because I was the same prior to 2007. After the Virginia Tech shooting though, I became hypersensitive to violence and could not bounce back as quickly. I was broken and lost the ability to shrug things off.

This time, it happened that a teacher was the hero, the one who wrestled the knife-wielding teenager to the ground. My half-eaten sandwich churned in my stomach at the notion of it. In the scenes playing out in my head, I was the coward, the one who rushed out of the room to safety while my students were left to fend for themselves. Despite my initial successes in therapy, I had quickly reverted back to my fearful old self, who was plagued by anxiety and struggling to hold on until the end of the semester. I was unarmed in the classroom, and I was absolutely powerless to stop a shooting, to stop my students from dying. The truth was I was not standing by the doorway with a chair in my hands. I stood helpless, the most obvious target, at the front of the room.

After reading the developing story, I realized I had started to cry. My breathing was shallow as though a panic attack was looming. I raced to the bathroom, thankful none of my colleagues were in the hallway. The last thing I needed was for someone to ask me if I was okay. Alone, I wept furiously. It was an ugly, messy cry that erupted from within, a tidal wave of emotion I had been carrying for months. I suppressed a wail, but my sniffles and gasps no doubt could be heard from the hallway if anyone were to pass by. I sobbed as I thought about the kids who were in that school in Pennsylvania, who would now carry the emotional scars from the battles being fought in our classrooms. It wasn't right that this type of violence had become commonplace.

As I calmed down, I looked in the mirror. My eyes were red and glazed over, resting on puffy dark circles. Under the fluorescent light, I looked exhausted, not just from crying, but from the nightmares keeping me awake every night for weeks. I looked ill. It was no wonder everyone asked if I was okay. I wasn't, but I had no control over my well-being. I was ill—*mentally* ill—and the treatment was doing little to help me. I grabbed some toilet paper, dabbed my eyes, and blew my nose. I turned on the faucet and scooped the cool water over my face in an attempt to wash away the sickness. Face dry, I returned to my office.

For the rest of the day, I attempted to stay off the internet, but every once in a while I caught myself returning for updates. I did my best to try to work, but, admittedly, I was worthless at that point.

In the days following the stabbing, my paranoia paralyzed me yet again.

I can't finish the semester. The weasel-faced boy is coming back to my class. I know he is. It's not safe, I kept saying to myself despite my attempts at reason. *I can't go back to that room.*

That room. The room with the masonry walls and worn-out carpet, with the stage at the front and the entrances on either side. The incident in Pennsylvania had reignited my terror from that cold and windy day in January when that stranger had entered my classroom. The weasel-faced boy was coming back. I became more and more certain my end was near.

Two weeks left in the semester, four classes in total—but there was no way I could enter that windowless classroom again. Instead, I worked around the clock over the next two days to create an end-of-term project that would require my class to meet in the computer lab for the remainder of the semester. Pedagogically, the project made a lot of sense—it was, after all, a course on computational methods for structural analysis—but I was simply trying to escape my fear. The computer lab was safer. The weasel-faced boy would not be able to find me and my students there. He would show up to our regular classroom with a gun in hand only to find the room empty. Even at the time, I knew it was ridiculous.

Logic told me the stranger was just a student who had rudely interrupted my class in January, but my illness convinced me he was a real threat. The incident in Pennsylvania only meant we were coming closer to an attack on me. I created the term project out of necessity. By that point, I was in survival mode.

That April, I received notice I had been selected for a national award for my excellence in teaching. I could not stomach the irony that I excelled at teaching despite the fact I was utterly terrified of it.

Reflections on Academia

May 2014

May rolled in like a gentle ocean wave, washing the beach of all debris and leaving the sand smooth and spotless as it receded. With the semester behind me, I was able to regroup and focus on my preparations for tenure. I had joined the faculty at the University of Michigan five years prior, knowing it would be a steep climb to tenure. At a top research university, tenure required excellence in research above all else. I also needed to be an outstanding teacher and perform service to my department, to the university, and to my professional community. However, teaching and service were always secondary to research. While the general criteria were straightforward, the actual metrics for success were rather nebulous. The fact was the definition of "excellence" varied from discipline to discipline, and even within a single discipline, "excellence" seemed to be a moving target.

To prepare for my tenure evaluation, I needed to assemble several things into a casebook, a portfolio that would allow the university to assess my performance during my time at the university. First, I needed to provide to my casebook committee a list of names of experts inside and outside the university who would write letters of evaluation of my performance. The external letters would carry the most weight in terms of my ability to run a world-class research program. I also needed to provide the names of undergraduate and graduate students who had taken my courses and who had worked under me in research. These letters would provide qualitative data on my ability to teach and advise students. Lastly, I needed to assemble a curriculum vitae documenting everything I had done in my professional career, including all the papers written, the presentations made, the grants brought in, the students advised, the courses taught, including my scores on teaching evaluations, the committees served on, and so on. The curriculum vitae was supplemented with one-page statements written by me about my impact in the areas of research, teaching, and service. All of this documentation would be evaluated by my department's executive committee, by the college's executive committee, by the provost, and then lastly approved by the university's Board of Regents. It was an intimidating process.

I was not worried about my accomplishments as a teacher because teaching came naturally to me despite my absolute fear of it. While I was generally a quiet and anxious person, I transformed into someone else completely when I stood at the front of the classroom. I had mastered the art of performance, speaking with confidence and clarity and mixing tedious theory with illustrative examples students could relate to. In grad school I discovered students learn best when they are actively engaged, and so I peppered my lectures with in-class activities requiring students to apply the abstract concepts.

Students appreciated my unique style to teaching, and my course evaluations were always at the top of my department. I loved working with students. Their bright and inquisitive minds, their ability to collectively see problems from all different angles, energized me. Their diverse perspectives gave me a deeper understanding of the material and made concepts I had seen a hundred times appear new.

I loved my field, too. I loved how life, at least within the realm of engineering, could be boiled down to neat little equations. Concepts were communicated in the language of calculus, and complex phenomena could nearly always be solved by computational methods. The classes I taught—and the research I did—involved a blend of computer programming and simulation, which I found to be more like a game than work. To solve a problem, you needed to come up with a strategy, type line after line of code, and then systematically debug the code to get it to run properly. Once debugged, the possibilities for exploration are limitless. I liked the challenge of troubleshooting, and over time, I became an expert diagnostician. Students would come to me with a broken code or a faulty computer model, and I knew how to ask the right questions that would lead them to identify the problems.

While I excelled in the classroom, my confidence, especially as a researcher and as a member of my professional community, shifted violently with my moods. When I was up, I was a superstar. My thoughts became razor-sharp, and my mind moved at lightning speed. Brilliant ideas zoomed past and, if I tried hard enough, I was able to capture a few of them. My activity level shot through the roof. I took on new projects and worked feverishly. In one week of mania, I derived the formulation for a new finite element, wrote a computer program to implement the element in commercial software, ran simulations to verify the formulation, and drafted a twenty-plus-page manuscript for publication—an effort that would have taken several months under normal circumstances. I did all of this the same week that I painted the walls of my bedroom, rearranged furniture, wrote reports to funding agencies, held my usual meetings, prepared notes for a new class I was teaching, and delivered lectures. When I was manic, superhuman powers gave me the ability to go at something with unparalleled intensity, clarity, and creativity, resulting in spectacular bursts of productivity. Understandably, I spoke of myself with inflated self-importance at those times, and I moved with a sureness prompting me to take risks and aggressively seek out opportunities. Not to mention, Susan couldn't deny I was a much greater help around the house during those times.

When I was down, though, I became a dismal failure. It did not help academia was a cruel place, one of ruthless competition and constant criticism. It was no secret funding was scarce, and I expected there would naturally be competition amongst research groups in the pursuit of discovery. However, I entered academia completely unaware of—and out of touch with—the old boys' network that dominated universities. Moreover, on more than one occasion, I was brought to tears by the ferocity of the competition. I made several critical mistakes in my first years as a professor without the proper mentorship, one of the costliest being the submission of poorly conceived manuscripts to the wrong journals. My first papers were rejected with horrendous and offensive comments from reviewers. I called Susan in tears after each and every rejection, and I questioned whether I should bother to continue my career path as an academic.

Being a young, queer woman in a male-dominated field left me further cast out. Not only did I have to battle the assumption I was a graduate student at every single conference I attended, I also had to fend off men who made inappropriate advances. I was fresh meat to be devoured by the sharks swimming all around and all too close to me. I attended conferences where the entertainment referenced male sexuality and keynote speakers made sexist jokes about their wives. I had to dodge sharp teeth and comments like, "What is a pretty lady like you doing here?" Often the only woman in the room, I asked myself, *Why would anyone willingly put herself through such torment?* It would have been so easy to give up, but in the end, I could not let myself be a statistic. The attrition rate of women in engineering—especially in academia—was abysmal, and I knew the only way things could improve was if more women stayed in the field. In the end, I decided to tough it out.

After being raked over the coals those first few years, things eventually improved. Through persistence, I secured some funding for my research and at the same time learned the art of writing a publishable journal paper. I began to study my academic community closely, paying careful attention to the key players within professional societies. I shook the hands of men who squeezed too hard, and I introduced myself despite their puzzled looks. I stood in rooms of a hundred people or more, again, mostly men, and defended my ideas presentation after presentation. I searched for committees to serve on, and, when the committee chairs asked for volunteers to serve on a task group or to do some other time-consuming work, I leaped at the opportunity, even volunteering to lead. As I made my way in, I held to a strategy of consistently doing good work in research and in service. It was not easy, but before long, I was invited to give talks, to collaborate, to serve on scientific committees, and to take on editorial duties. There is no doubt I was successful in my field by the time I came up for tenure, but the question was, was it enough?

That May, as I filled in the various sections of the casebook, my shortcomings became pathetically obvious to me. Despite my stellar ratings on my course evaluations, the critical comments from the few students who were dissatisfied with my courses echoed in my head. What if one of them was asked to write a letter of evaluation? Gaps, where rejected papers should have been accepted, glared at me when I studied my list of publications. Any evaluator would see that the accepted papers were weak, and the number of papers was certainly not enough. Looking at the grants awarded, I remembered all the unsuccessful proposals returned with harsh comments. I read and reread my casebook, the disappointment and disgust creeping up on me and then filling my stomach with lead. A compilation of failures. My colleagues assured me I would be fine going through tenure, but they would feel differently if they had actually studied my casebook.

My doubts about tenure set a fire under me. In my desperation, I became determined to stop sleeping and work tirelessly to churn out publications. After all, I had written journal papers from conception to completion in a week's time, albeit while manic. As a result, I forced myself to sleep each night only to awaken at three o'clock in the morning. Instead of trying to go back to sleep, I would brew a pot of coffee and pull out my laptop. I needed more papers. The only way to make it happen was to run some computer simulations and write the manuscripts as fast as I could. One or two more papers submitted by the end of May would give them a reasonable chance of being accepted in time to be counted towards tenure. But as my productivity spiked, things started to become weird. Despite my religious dedication to swallowing my medication cocktail every day, it wasn't long before I started to hear voices again.

Shanghai

June 2014

The scene felt all too familiar. Afraid of missing my flight, I had arrived at the airport nearly three hours before departure. Like any seasoned traveler, my behavior at the airport was almost ritualistic. While newcomers fumbled with their belongings in the security line, I stood by impatiently with my shoes in hand, liquids stuffed into a quart-sized Ziploc baggy, and my laptop prepared for the gray plastic bins. Once I made it through security, I stopped at the newsstand, where I bought a bottle of water and a bag of chips, not because I was thirsty or hungry, but because I was afraid of being stuck on the plane without nourishment. Something about being confined to a plane, constrained to my seat, was unsettling. I then proceeded to my gate, where I waited patiently for boarding. Rather than try to get some work done, I used the spare time to clear my head.

"Attention all passengers on Delta Flight two sixty-nine to Shanghai. We will begin boarding in a moment. Please have your passport and boarding pass ready."

The passengers crowded the gate while I slipped my journal into my backpack and pulled out my travel documents. It was my first time going to mainland China, and I was rather excited. It helped that I was swinging into mania. I had spent the previous evening at a conference in Las Vegas where I was presented with an award for a paper I had published with my students. Next stop, Shanghai to attend a conference where my students were presenting. I would only be in Shanghai a few days because I had to get back to the Midwest for yet another conference. I had a knack of double- (or, in this case, triple-) booking myself for conferences in a single week. Nonetheless, travel to three different conferences in three different time zones in the span of ten days was ludicrous, even for me. However, the fact that the stress and lack of sleep would trigger a manic episode was one of the things I secretly enjoyed about travel. While I pretended I was dreading the crazy Vegas-Shanghai-Indianapolis trip, I was actually looking forward to it, so much so that in my pre-trip excitement I abruptly decided to cut my dose of Zyprexa in half. While I had never before meddled with my medication, I rationalized there was no room for a cloudy mind on such a major trip; I needed to be "on." The day in Vegas, I felt *alive*. By the time I arrived in Shanghai, I was *on fire*.

The plane landed at the Shanghai-Pudong airport late in the evening. The exhaustion was real, and rather than trusting my mind to get me to the right place by public transit after the fourteen-hour journey, I opted for a taxi. The driver spoke no English so I showed him a printout with the hotel address, hoping he would know how to get me to my destination. He nodded, muttered something, and drove off wildly. We sped down the highway, weaving in and out of traffic, and by the time we arrived in the neighborhood of my hotel, my knuckles were sore from gripping the door handle. I ventured down the last block toward the hotel with my suitcase in tow while the sidewalks bustled with activity. Despite that it was nearly midnight, the family-owned shops lining the street were still open, and in one shop, a woman bartered passionately with the storeowner about the price of some dishes. Honking assaulted my ears as cars, bikes, and scooters swerved in every direction, the motorbike engines filling the air with the strong scent of gasoline.

In my cozy hotel room, despite the long journey, my eyes remained wide open. My stomach clenched and growled, but I had promised Rachel I would not wander the city streets. Plus, I had no idea what to look for in Shanghai anyway. Restaurants serving Western cuisine were likely nowhere to be found, and, regardless, I doubted I would be able to communicate well enough with the locals to request a vegetarian meal. Instead, I put on my pajamas, turned out the light, and resigned to a night of tossing in bed.

The conference in Shanghai was one of the biggest international conferences in my field. I had spent my first few years as an assistant professor trying to make my way into the structural fire engineering community. I built off of the research I pursued as a Ph.D. student, which was loosely inspired by the fire-induced collapses of the World Trade Center Towers. I aspired to make buildings safer against catastrophic fires, and I did so by introducing innovative models that more accurately simulated structural response in fire. Over time, I had made connections with researchers from all over the world, and I was comforted by how many people I knew at the conference. Unlike my usual quiet and anxious self, I had no hesitations about walking up to people I barely knew and offering a handshake. Having just been handed a prestigious award in Vegas, my self-esteem bloomed. The grandiosity of mania further inflated my self-importance, an indispensable feeling because I spent most of my time outside of mania doubting and loathing myself.

During a break between sessions, I walked to the refreshment table and filled a mug with coffee. I turned around to find a smiling young man rocking eagerly on his heels.

"Professor Jeffers?" he asked.

"Yes?" I said uncertainly. I had never met him before, and I was caught off guard by the fact he knew who I was.

"It's such an honor to meet you." He shook my hand warmly. "My name is Gaurav Chaudhary. I am a Ph.D. student of Dr. Lin's. I am working on modeling the behavior of composite floor systems in fire using finite element analysis. I have read your papers."

"Ah, yes," I said. Dr. Lin was one of the most well-known researchers in the field of structural fire engineering. He and I had talked at a conference before, but he was not a close acquaintance of mine. I had long admired his work and hoped one day my work would reach the same status as his. The fact that one of his students had studied some of my papers took me by surprise.

The student continued. "The work you did on the fiber element approach was really impressive."

"Well, thank you." He had not only read my work, but he

actually thought it was *good*. He looked back at me with his star-struck eyes.

"I don't want to keep you. I know you are a very busy person," he said. "It was an honor to meet you."

He shook my hand again and walked off.

When I got back to my hotel room that evening, I was beaming. I tossed my backpack and nametag, and jumped around the room, swinging my fists wildly in the air and whisper-shouting, "Yes-yes-yes!" I had been to countless conferences where I introduced myself as a nobody to people more senior. Now, finally, someone had heard of me and had even read my papers. All of my insecurities dissolved. I was unstoppable. I was invincible. I was a superstar.

I pulled out a pad of paper and began jotting down the ideas I had generated at the conference so far. Possible collaborations. New leads on papers to read. Ideas for proposals. Possibilities for my students to consider in their work. In fifteen minutes, I had filled the sheet of paper with bulleted lists, ideas starred and underlined, questions written off to the side, and snippets of text linked with arrows spreading across the page. That single burst of activity was worth hours of hard effort.

The rest was, per usual, filled with long days of boring presentations about the same boring topics in a large, sleepy lecture hall set a few degrees too warm. While at times I thought my research field was exciting, today I was irritated with how slow research progressed. Few people seemed to be doing work that was truly innovative. Every research presentation was a snail's crawl from its status at the same conference two years ago. Overnight, I had grown tired from the travel, and the magic from the first day of the conference had dissolved.

Questioning the merits of others' research led me to question the merits of my own research. My students and I were certainly doing things differently, but we strived for novelty at the expense of rigor. We often trod in territory we lacked expertise in. Consequently, our analyses ended up being far too simplistic to be applicable to real life. My conversation with Gaurav aside, it seemed like no one had an interest in building on my group's work. I had received almost no citations on the papers I had published, which meant most people were not reading my papers or they did not think my work was good enough to reference in their work. It made me look pathetic in comparison to my peers at the University of Michigan who had citations through the roof.

As I sat in the lecture hall, my brow beaded with sweat as fears trickled in that my students, Blake and Diya, would make mistakes in their presentations or be challenged with difficult questions from the audience. Critical comments from the people in the audience—people who had surely reviewed my papers—resounded in my mind. While most reviewers were professional, I couldn't help but take their comments on my research methods personally. To know that the room of more than one hundred people was watching my students' presentations and *judging* them—judging *me*—was unsettling. Moreover, it was possible at least one of the members of the audience would be writing a letter of evaluation for my tenure. A lot was at stake.

Blake's presentation was first. He spoke with a confidence that would convince anyone of the value of his work. We had practiced the presentation before leaving Ann Arbor, and it was clear he had run through it several times since. Diya spoke more softly—a cultural difference between her and Blake—but her command of technical details was phenomenal. When asked questions after the presentation, she gave answers that would transcend some seasoned professors. My team worked hard, and their accomplishments shone through their presentations.

Despite the relief that followed my students' presentations, I left the conference feeling embarrassed. It was like emotional whiplash going from the highest of highs to the lowest of lows in the span of a day. With the change in mood, I faced a new reality that I did not belong amongst this community of scholars. I was insignificant, inferior, and flawed in every way. A complete and utter failure. It was the price I paid for the brief euphoria accompanying mania. The lack of sleep caught up with me, my thoughts becoming less and less rational. I was still "up" in the sense that I couldn't sleep or calm myself, but my thoughts were darkening. In another day, I felt the skin-crawling feeling of a mixed episode coming on.

On the final evening of the conference, a couple of students from Tongji University offered to take Blake, Diya, and me to the Bund, a famous promenade along the Huangpu River. After a short taxi ride from the conference center, we pushed through the crowd to get a complete view of the neon-lighted skyline of Shanghai. Brilliant, intricate patterns lit up the buildings, changing color and form with each passing moment. The city seemed so modern compared to cities I had visited previously. It was a glimpse of the technological boom in China in recent years, a sign of a flourishing economy. Around us, hundreds of people walked in all directions. Tourists snapping photos, lovers holding hands, friends laughing in each other's company. I had always felt comfortable in the presence of my students, but in that moment, I had never felt more isolated and alone.

"There is a restaurant close by that has a terrace with a very nice view of the city. Would you like to go there and have a drink?" asked Xiao, one of the Tongji students who was leading our little tour of Shanghai.

I looked at Blake and Diya, both enthusiastic about the idea.

"Sure," I said in agreement.

Ornate décor spiraled along the walls, ceiling, and floor of the Victorian hotel—a long-standing symbol of great prosperity. Photos of famous people who had stayed at the hotel, including former U.S. presidents and movie stars, adorned the hallway from the atrium to the elevator. It was a place where only the extremely wealthy and famous stayed. Our group—entirely made up of students except for me—was out of place, which made the whole thing even more exciting.

We sat around a table on the sixth-floor terrace, ordered a bottle of wine, and split it evenly between the five of us. In contrast to the hotel's entryway, the restaurant had a modern design.

"Dr. Jeffers, what did you think of the presentation on localized fires?" Diya asked.

"I found it interesting. It's similar to the work Blake is doing, but our focus is more on the structural response whereas theirs was more on the fire dynamics," I replied, playing the role of a professor who had it all together. "What do you think, Blake, do you think you could use their fire model in your analyses?"

"I think so," he said.

"So you'll have that finished by August, right?" I joked.

"Yeah, *totally*," Blake said sarcastically. It was a classic joke between a student and his advisor. Professors tended to be uncharacteristically demanding and set unrealistic expectations of their students, decimating the student's self-worth and resulting in them working twenty-four hours a day in the subpar conditions of graduate student office space. I was actually one of the most compassionate and flexible advisors in the department, and my students knew and appreciated it, but still, I joked about the power dynamic.

We talked for some time, and as our glasses emptied, we moved to the edge of the terrace to take in the views of the city and the plaza below. The conversation between us faded. My students may have been thinking about what an amazing opportunity it was to travel to China. Recalling my first international experiences as a teenager living in Frankfurt, Germany, I could understand how life-altering the exposure to a different culture could be. Being here at the Bund amid the Shanghai skyline, sipping wine at a high-end hotel was quite the experience.

I tried to take in the artificial beauty of the surrounding

buildings with a lens of appreciation, but I couldn't overcome the darkness that had been distorting my thoughts in recent days. I tried to fight the negativity with logic—to tell myself to enjoy this unique opportunity—but the hateful thoughts crept in.

You are worthless.

You are alone.

You are a failure.

You are an embarrassment.

You are a fraud.

You do not even deserve to live.

The dialogue grew louder until an image flashed in my mind.

I climbed over the railing and stood on the ledge above the crowd of people. I felt dizzy as I looked down from such a great height. My mind teetered. *Do it, don't do it, do it, don't do it. Failure*, the words ricocheted around my skull. *Alone. Worthless.* Again, again. *Embarrassment. Fraud.* Enough!

Fuck it.

I closed my eyes and jumped. The wind rushed past me. I flew through the air. I was a motorcycle on a highway, a four-wheeler on the main road. Butterflies filled my gut as I became weightless. I was woozy with the feeling of imminent death coming closer, closer. And, in an instant, I slammed into the pavement below. I could feel the pain as every bone in my body shattered. And then the world faded to black—

"Dr. Jeffers?"

I started at the sound of my name.

"Dr. Jeffers, are you ready to go?"

The students had gathered and were ready to leave the restaurant.

"Uh, yeah," I said as normally as I could. My face was pale from the lack of oxygen, and my body was shaking. I took one more look over the railing, shuddered, and then followed the students to the elevator. Xiao hailed a taxi for me and directed it to my hotel. Blake and Diya were staying in another hotel. I rode in silence, stunned by the realness of my vision of suicide. When I got back to my hotel room, I cried myself to sleep.

Home Again

June 2014

"Mama! Mama!" Skye cheered as I walked in the door. I dropped my bags in the entryway and forced a smile for her. My eyes were bleary from the fourteen-hour flights and thirteen-hour time differences. My mind swelled and buzzed with a mixture of exhaustion, physical discomfort, and a mild hangover from the free drinks on the flight. On such long trips, I had trouble regulating my coffee and alcohol intake, mostly because I never knew when I should be sleeping and when I should be awake. Whenever the flight attendant came by with a refill, whether coffee or wine, I had a habit of saying "yes." Only when the plane reached the ground did I feel regret for my decisions.

I dug through my bags to find the goodies I had picked up as souvenirs: a light-up watch for Skye and a wall decoration for Susan.

"I got you something," I teased Skye as I held the watch behind my back.

"What is it?" She ran to me, her little arms in the air grabbing for anything and everything.

I pulled out the watch and pushed the button on the side of

the watch, making the face light up.

"Whoa!" She grabbed the watch and ran to her bedroom so that she could see it light up in the dark.

"I got something for you too," I said to Susan with a smile. Though I knew that I had to depart for Indianapolis the next day, I felt warm and safe at home. Being in Susan's company was like hitting the reset button.

"How was the conference?" she asked.

I could not tell her that I had spent the previous evening thinking about leaping off the sixth-floor terrace at a hotel, so instead, I focused on the positive moments from the conference. I said, "It was great. Diya and Blake did an awesome job. They got lots of questions from the audience, and afterward several people told me that my students were doing good work."

"Of course." Susan never doubted my abilities the way I did.

"And I achieved rock-star status at this conference. There was a Ph.D. student working with Dr. Lin who actually knew who I was. He had even read my work. And he actually thought it was good. I thought he was going to ask for my autograph," I joked. It was surreal reflecting on how great I had felt at the start. While I couldn't mention it to Susan, the disturbing moment on the terrace overshadowed the whole conference. I pushed the negative experience from my mind and kept my focus on Susan.

"Oh yeah?" she said. Her voice had suddenly become cool. I could not tell if she was bored from hearing me talk about how awesome I was or if she was just stressed from having been left home alone to take care of Skye while I traveled the world. I was too exhausted to argue, so I decided to change the subject.

"How are you?"

"It's been really stressful," she said.

"Tell me about it."

"Skye hasn't been sleeping again." She rested her forehead on her fist, presumably trying to fight the tears. "She was up late every night until after eleven, and then she was up by six most days. I gave her her tablet and tried to get some sleep, but she didn't let me. By the time we got ready and got out the door, it was already after nine, and then with my commute, I didn't get to work until almost eleven. It was pointless because I had to leave by four to pick her up from daycare."

"That's rough." There was nothing I could say to make it any better.

"Then I took her to the store, and she didn't tell me she had to go to the bathroom. She had an accident, and I didn't even have clothes for her to change into. It was awful."

She was clearly overwhelmed. I could not help feeling terrible I had to leave the next day for Indiana. My job was amazing in the sense that I had a unique opportunity to travel the world. I had been all over Europe, Asia, Africa, and North America, seeing things most people could only dream of. But it came at a cost. I could not have a job and a family unless I had a supportive wife at home. When I thought of it like that, I felt more like a man than a woman. I had grown up in a home in which my dad worked the "important" engineering job, while my mom was stuck at home with three kids. Even when she went to college and received a degree in teaching, her status was always secondary to my dad's. I hated the inequality between my parents, but here I was reliving it through my own career and my relationship with Susan.

All I could say was, "I'm sorry." Then, I added, "I wish I didn't have to leave tomorrow for Indiana."

"Well, I'm going to bed." Susan got up from the couch without saying any more and proceeded to get ready for bed.

My head spun. I didn't want to leave her all alone, but travel was part of my job. I had to go to these conferences to present my research and network with colleagues and receive awards. In addition, I was struggling and hurt that I didn't get to talk about my vision of leaping off the building. The experience really shook me, and I had no way of processing it. I would tell Rachel when I saw her in a couple weeks, but a couple weeks seemed like an eternity to keep it inside.

I put Skye down for bed, which took a good hour, and then I snuck into the bedroom. Susan was silent, either sleeping or faking it. I lay down in the darkness without so much as a kiss goodnight.

Summer Blues

July 2014

The sun shone through the trees, casting spiderwebs in the smudges of my filthy windshield. It was mid-morning, much later than my usual arrival to work. My summer schedule left nothing to look forward to, no order, and no consistency in my days. It was at those times I relied heavily on self-discipline. One would think four months void of interruption would yield wondrous creativity and productivity for an academic. However, it was at those times I became the most lost. With nothing to hold me accountable, I was a master of wasting time. And the wasting of time made me feel like a failure. And the guilt of failure stalled any productivity and destroyed my self-worth. And so I wasted more time, and the cycle perpetuated.

On this particular morning, I could not overcome the inertia that was holding me down. The weight of all the things I had failed to accomplish over the past two months was immeasurable. I could not write. Since that moment at the conference, I had no desire to develop fresh ideas for papers or proposals. I stopped responding to emails. I avoided meetings. Even casual encounters in the hallway at work made me feel nauseated. I shied away from my office, telling myself I would be more productive if I worked in the comforts of my home, but when I stayed home, I lay on the couch for hours at a time, incapable of doing anything. I was tired of life. I was tired of being me. My entire experience on the Vegas-Shanghai-Indianapolis trip had been wiped from my memory and replaced by a feeling of failure that stretched infinitely in all directions.

I parked the car in the student lot and turned off the engine. I sat paralyzed behind the steering wheel.

"I have to go to the office today," I said under my breath. "I *need* to work."

I knew I would feel better if I could just accomplish *something*. After all, I had been here so many times before. The accomplishment of one task would lead to another, and, if I committed to working for just one afternoon, I might be able to break the cycle. Tenure was looming, and while my casebook had already been sent out to senior colleagues at peer institutions who would write the ever-so-important letters of evaluation, I was expected to give a final push to get as much on my CV as possible before it moved to the College of Engineering in November. But just like so many days before, my half-hearted pep talk proved futile; I was trapped behind my steering wheel, anchored beneath the suffocation of failure.

Maybe if I take a short nap.

I was awfully tired these days. Unlike my usual self, I had trouble waking up in the mornings. I drank coffee like it was water, and I napped an hour or more each afternoon. I was in bed by nine o'clock each night and, in fact, I slept so much that

Susan complained it was all I did anymore. The housework piled up. Dishes overfilled the sink, and laundry poured out of every basket in the house. I was not carrying my weight at home, and Susan was becoming frustrated with me. She had no idea that I was not carrying my weight at work either. My failures were secrets I kept hidden within the shadows of my shame and embarrassment.

I locked the doors, cracked the window, and leaned my seat all the way back. I grabbed a sweatshirt from the passenger seat and balled it up under my head like a pillow. I set the alarm on my phone so that I would wake up in time for my eleven o'clock meeting, and then I closed my eyes. I thought only briefly about the possibility that one of my students might see me—Professor Ann E. Jeffers—sleeping in my van, but I quickly dismissed the thought. I did not care if anyone saw me; there was no sense in trying to hide the fact that I was a complete waste.

I lay in an unusual state in which I was not awake but not quite asleep either. I squirmed every now and then in an attempt to get comfortable, and I breathed deeply, hoping I could attain that restful feeling one gets with a successful nap. But it was useless. I could not shake the feeling of insomnia that comes when you drink a big cup of coffee at bedtime. I was buzzing and restless.

As my frustrations grew, I looked at my clock. A jolt shot through me. An hour had passed and I still had not slept. My alarm was set to go off in another minute.

"Shit," I said. I felt no better than when I lay down. I lifted my seat and gripped the steering wheel, wondering what to do next. *I don't want to work, but I need to work*. I couldn't move.

"Shit, shit, shit!" I pounded the steering wheel in an attempt to bully myself out of the seat. *Just* go *to your office*.

But it was useless.

With overwhelming guilt, I grabbed my phone and pulled up the Gmail app. "Something has come up and I can't make it to the office today," I typed. "Can we reschedule for next week?" I was canceling on one of my students.

I tried to rationalize that depression might justify a sick day from work—mental illness was after all an *illness*—but the problem was that this behavior had become routine for me. I was dropping the ball every time I turned around. I could not even count the times I had canceled on my students for the same pathetic reason in recent months. Not only was I ruining myself, I was also hurting their progress, and the worst part was it felt like I was doing it intentionally.

Nonetheless, I started the engine and backed out of my parking spot. Taking a day off, I should do something fun or enjoyable—maybe treat myself to a movie or do some shopping. After all, Rachel was always insisting I do some self-care. But instead, I got on the highway and, as tears filled the corners of my eyes, I drove home.

Pathetic. Worthless. Failure. Run yourself into the ground.

At home, I walked up the stairs, the sun burning through the picture window in the living room. I fell on the couch, closed my eyes, and tried to silence the dreadful dialogue in my head. I lay somewhere between awake and asleep for four hours and then I pulled myself from the couch and drove back to Ann Arbor to pick up Skye from daycare.

Therapy (Part 3)

July 2014

"Hi, Ann. How are you?" Rachel asked cheerfully as she stood at the entrance of the waiting room.

"Good, and how are you?" I said politely.

"Good. Come on back." She escorted me downstairs to the relative safety of her office, and I took a seat on the couch.

"So how are things?" she asked, knowing that I could let down my front now.

"I don't know," I said, and, just like that, the tears started to flow. I had called her earlier in the week to tell her that I was having a difficult time. My mood had come down hard following the conferences, and I was especially distraught about the suicidal thoughts I had had in Shanghai.

She grabbed a box of tissues from the end table and handed them to me. It was part of our routine. Each week, I came to her office all teary-eyed, and, instead of having the tissues in reach, she made it a point to hand them to me. I had almost begun to expect it from her.

After wiping my nose, I sniffled. "I just don't know anymore. I mean, I was at the conference and things were going so well and then—boom—I'm standing at the railing of the sixth floor of a hotel, and I'm envisioning myself jumping."

I began to cry and was unable to continue. Rachel looked at me and said, "But you didn't jump."

"I know." I sniffled again and wiped my nose. "But it was so real. I mean, I could feel myself falling and slamming into the pavement. It was scary. And it makes me afraid of myself. I was able to control it this time—I mean, I didn't jump—but what about next time? I just don't understand where these thoughts come from. It's not like I want to die." I paused, trying to figure how I felt in the present. "And now, today, I'm fine."

"And what about any hallucinations? Paranoia?"

"I've been hearing the static and whispering," I replied. "And when I took out the trash the other day, I was pretty sure there was someone lurking in the shadows. But I know that no one was there. I mean, I live in the middle of nowhere."

"I think you need to let Dr. Park know about these things. When do you see her again?"

"Monday." We were approaching the end of the week; surely, Monday would come quickly.

"Okay, good. Is there anything you want me to tell her?"

"No, I've got it."

I walked out of Rachel's office feeling not the least bit better about the way things were going.

Monday came around slowly. The depression was heavy like a cast-iron skillet.

My fifteen-minute med checks with Dr. Park had become predictable. Mood? Unstable. Hallucinations? Check. Paranoia? Check. Thoughts of hurting self? Check. Let's increase the dose of X and add Y.

This time, my Zyprexa was replaced with another antipsychotic medication, Abilify.

Maybe this one will work. On the way home, I had the prescription filled, and I suppressed a small hope that this one might be the right one.

Psychosis

July 2014

My body buzzed with an energy I had never felt before. I could see in such high definition that I could even make out the atoms and molecules that made up matter. Edges were sharp. Colors were brilliant. Contrasts were emphasized. The world was absolutely beautiful. My heart beat with life. No, it didn't just beat; it *boomed*. I was alive. God, I was alive. My mind was swarming so much that I could not formulate a single thought. I tried to slow it down but I had absolutely no control. It was like trying to reason with myself while in a dream. Even when I was able to distill a single thought from my brain, I was unable to articulate it. It was as if the thought was on the edge of my mind, ready to be spoken but lacking definition. More like a feeling than a concept. A know-it-when-I-see-it kind of feeling.

I folded laundry in the bedroom while Susan put Skye to bed. She had stepped in to care for Skye because I'd grown impatient. I was asking Skye to put her pajamas on, and, because she did not get dressed the very second that I asked her to, I began to lose my cool. Susan sensed my irritability right away and calmly entered the room. I knew it was time for me to walk away. We were an excellent team in that regard.

I put the energy to good use. I could not generate a rational thought, but I could do manual labor. Folding laundry was mindless. Moreover, it was productive. I had not been doing my fair share of housework. I tried to help when I could, but unfortunately, that was not very often.

The buzz from the air conditioner outside the window gave off a background noise that helped to calm me. It blocked the dialogue from Susan and Skye, allowing me to find some peace. It was a kind of meditation that I was doing: folding laundry, breathing deeply, and listening to the hum of the air conditioner as I cleared my mind.

But my mind was not right. I could not find serenity. The noise grew louder. It was not the sound of the air conditioner; it was the sound of music. Digital music. Like the kind of music you would hear in a Nintendo game from the 1990s. But it wasn't the Super Mario theme song. It was the sound of a player piano blasting a tune from an Old Western film. A digital saloon. Coming from my bedroom wall.

I paused.

Is this real?

It was odd. It was very odd. So odd it most certainly could not be real. My heart was pounding because I already knew the answer to the question.

Okay. If it is in my mind, I will still hear it when I step into the next room.

I put the laundry down and stepped into the hallway. I came back into the room. Back and forth between the hallway and bedroom. The music not only continued, but it grew to a thunder.

In a panic, I ran out of the bedroom and into the living room, where it was quiet. I breathed heavily and tried to bring myself back down. The music had stopped, which gave me a feeling of relief. But I was still buzzing. Atoms and molecules. I could not compose atoms and molecules into a single comprehensible thought. I looked inwardly and saw nothingness. I was losing my sense of self. An etching in the sand being eroded by the breeze. The panic was sneaking in, faster and faster. I jumped as I heard muffled voices coming from outside. There were people out there. Outside, in my yard. At night. People in my yard.

Wait. No. We live in the middle of nowhere. People would not be in my yard, especially at this time of day. None of this is making sense.

I knew it was psychosis. Auditory hallucinations. I was hearing music and voices that were not real.

There was only one thing left to do. I ran back to the bedroom, closed the door, turned out the light, and pulled the covers over my head. Images passed through my mind at lightning speed. Faces. Strange faces. Menacing faces. Demons. Blood. Gore.

And the next thing I knew, I had fallen asleep.

Vacationing with Mental Illness

July 2014

Susan and I had been up and down the East Coast in our time together, but we had never been to Charleston, South Carolina. When planning our vacation, we knew that we wanted to reach the ocean, but the "where" was always difficult. Since we had moved to Michigan, we hardly ever made it to the coast because the drive was not practical. This was tragic because the beach had been instrumental in my healing during my time at Virginia Tech. It did not matter how horrible I felt, all we needed to do was pack the car and drive the four hours to the beach, where I could wrestle with the waves until I was exhausted and felt at peace. We did not have the luxury of hopping in the car and driving to the beach once we moved to Michigan, although later I would come to learn Michigan beaches were nearly as spectacular as the ocean.

The drive from our home to Charleston was thirteen hours at best. A small child in the backseat and standstill construction traffic added another three hours. It was a painful sacrifice but one worth making as I held hopes the sun, sand,

and waves might cure some of my madness.

We got off to an early start, Susan in the driver's seat and I riding co-pilot, Skye in the back in her car seat. It was our usual set-up, as Susan was the better driver and I the better navigator. When we flipped roles, I became spacey and untalkative, while Susan got irritable and carsick while managing the music, snacks, and GPS. As we made our way into Ohio, we chatted about Susan's job.

Susan finished sharing a story about a conflict that arose between her and one of her colleagues. I saw an opportunity to update her on my mental health. It was an unexpected shift in the conversation, but I needed to let her know the psychosis was worsening. I generally tried not to share too much too often because I didn't want to overwhelm her.

"My doctor switched my antipsychotic last week," I said, carefully eying Susan's reaction.

She kept her eyes fixed on the road. "Is it working?"

"Well, not exactly." I didn't want to tell her outright about the hallucinations, so I tried to buy time. "I mean, it takes time for the medication to take effect."

"Of course."

There was an awkward pause. Then, gripping the armrest, I said, "I heard music coming from the walls the other night."

"What do you mean?" Her hands remained steady on the steering wheel, but the glance toward me looked unsettled.

"I was folding laundry, and I felt off. The air conditioner was running, and I heard music coming from the walls. It was digital music, like you would hear in a Nintendo game, but it was playing the tune of a player piano from the Old West."

"Oh." Susan kept her head forward, but I could tell she was uncomfortable with what I had just shared. Eventually, she said, "Are you sure it wasn't something else? Me and Skye talking in the other room, or—"

"No. I know what I heard."

In her usual way of seeking reason, she asked, "What did you do?"

"I stepped into the hallway, and the music stopped. When I went back in the bedroom again, it was playing even louder. So I ran down the hallway to the living room."

"Well, I guess that's good." She glanced over at me and attempted a smile.

"That's not all." I shifted in my seat.

"Oh?" The smile disappeared from her face, and she fixed her eyes on the road.

"When I got to the living room, there were people outside in our yard. I was paranoid as hell."

"You saw them?" she asked with eyes wide.

"Not exactly. I heard them and I just knew they were out there." I hated having to explain the psychosis to Susan. Even though her intentions were good, the questioning and the looks of surprise were a little infantilizing. Proving there was a sliver of sanity left in me, I said, "Of course, the people outside weren't real."

Having finished sharing the details of what I had experienced, I relaxed my grip on the arm rest and took a deep breath.

"Did you tell your doctor about it?"

"Not yet." I hadn't had an appointment with Dr. Park yet

since starting the Abilify, but I would bring it up when I saw her next.

"Well, you might be right that you just need to give the medication time."

"Yeah," I said. "Plus, I didn't want to go through another med change before our vacation. I want this to be a good trip." I smiled half-heartedly.

"It will be good. We're going to have fun, digging in the sand and relaxing on the beach. Plus, I got us a sweet house for the week."

"That sounds awesome," I said, and then I switched the direction of the conversation. "What do you want to listen to next?" I picked up the book of CDs from the floor.

It was lunchtime when we arrived in Columbus. As a family of vegetarians, we decided our meals not based on what we were in the mood for, but rather on what was available to us. Our top pick of restaurants was always the place that had something on the menu besides fries and a side salad. Using my phone, I found a trendy place serving veggie sandwiches and pizza. It was out of our way, but good food was always worth the sacrifice.

We drove around the block several times to find street parking and then climbed out of the van with stiff legs. The inside of the restaurant was modern, with a fresh coat of lime-colored paint and lights that dangled from the ceiling. The hostess sat us in a booth and handed us a couple of sticky menus. She grabbed a kids' menu and a few crayons for Skye, who began scribbling something indiscernible.

"Skye, what do you want to eat?" I asked.

"French fries."

"You can't just eat French fries. You need to eat something else."

Still scribbling, she said simply, "Ketchup."

I tried to suppress a laugh at her cuteness. "If I order pizza, will you eat some of it?"

After some whining, she finally conceded. I knew it meant she would eat French fries doused in ketchup plus one bite of pizza. Still, it was variety. As parents, we had learned to pick our battles.

The crayons ran their course, and Skye started to get antsy. "Where's our food?" she asked repeatedly. We were in a rush to get back on the road, but the food was taking a long time to come out. Just as Susan was about to ask the server what the hold-up was, the food was brought to the table with steam rising from the pizza's melted cheese. Susan's veggie burger was to her liking, and Skye grinned at her exceptionally large basket of fries.

After allowing the pizza to cool a minute, I served a slice to Skye and two slices to myself. The pizza looked delicious, but as I took my first bite, I became ill with the feeling that there was meat in the pizza. Reminding myself that I had ordered a cheese pizza, I took a second bite.

Meat! Someone has ground up meat and blended it in the sauce. They are trying to poison you. You know that it is meat. Pepperoni pureed underneath the cheese. Hidden so that you won't find it.

I put the pizza slice down.

"Everything okay?" Susan asked when she realized that I was staring at the pizza instead of eating it.

"Uh, yeah, it's fine. Just a little hot," I said.

It was ludicrous to think that someone had poisoned my meal by slipping meat into the pizza. I tried to think who would do something like that and why, and I could think of no rational reason.

I took another bite. The image of ground flesh came to my mind, causing my stomach to turn.

Meat. It's definitely meat.

I took another bite and, despite the sickening taste, forced it down. I used logic to reason my way through it; there was no way that a person would grind up pepperoni and hide it in the sauce, especially at a vegetarian-friendly restaurant. Although I was certain I would get sick after eating the contaminated food, I was able to finish the two slices. It was a stupid thought, so I did not tell Susan about it.

We paid our check, climbed back into the van, and continued our long drive. The flat Midwest bubbled up into mountains, and the highway bent into steep curves. The scenery was a reminder of home—my home in hilly Pennsylvania and Susan's home in mountainous West Virginia. Hours later, the winding hills flattened and straightened. We had reached the Carolinas.

Skye was becoming impatient in the backseat. "Mama, are we there yet?" she whined.

"We're almost there, kiddo," I promised, but she groaned.

We arrived at the rental house at dusk, Susan and I tired and weary while Skye ran from room to room like a three-year-old who had napped all day in the car.

"Mama, have you *seen* my room?" she shouted, as she followed me into the master bedroom. "It's enormous, and it even has a ceiling fan!"

I laughed. "That's great. Hey, why don't you get your room set up for bedtime?"

Even with Skye's burst of energy, she quickly tired. We got her to settle down and watch a show on her tablet, Skye quickly drifting into sleep.

While Susan and I were tired, it was difficult to unwind after having been in the car for so long. Susan turned on the TV and flipped the channel until she found *The Golden Girls*, an all-time classic and my favorite show to fall asleep to. I closed my eyes, listening to the familiar voices of Dorothy, Rose, Blanche, and Sophia. Then, somewhere, a door opened. Footsteps sounded in the house.

It is a man. He's coming upstairs. To kill us.

My heart beat faster, and I jolted up. "Susan, did you hear that?"

"What?" she asked, still sleepily watching the TV.

"There's someone in the house. I heard footsteps. Someone has broken in." My breathing came more rapidly, and my skin prickled with urgency. "We need to get Skye to safety."

She calmly looked over from the TV. "There's no one here, but if you want me to go check, I will." It was an unusual switch in roles. Under normal circumstances, it was Susan who feared intruders and me who fearlessly snuck through the dark house to verify no one was there. Regardless, I was thankful she kept a level head and did not feed off my anxiety. I had no reservations taking up her heroic offer.

"Yes, please do."

Slowly, she opened the door and stepped out into the hallway. Wrapped tightly under the blanket, I breathed heavily in anticipation of a confrontation, but after a minute Susan came back, calm and unfazed.

"It's fine. There's no one here."

"Did you check on Skye?"

"Yes, she's fast asleep."

The tears came hard and fast. I inhaled deeply and sniffled. "I was *convinced* that someone was in here. Someone had broken in and was going to kill Skye. I heard the door open and the footsteps in the house." I clenched my fists to stop from trembling.

"Oh, Ann. I'm so sorry. No one is here, I promise. Skye is safe. And if someone came in here to hurt Skye or us, he would have to get through me first," Susan said reassuringly.

I smiled. "You're right. It was just so real." I paused. "I hate that I am so unwell."

"You've got this. You just need to find the right medication. And you are doing that."

She gave me a hug, and with that, I finally slept.

The next few days were slow and calming. We wandered lazily along the beach, pausing to build towering sandcastles and dive into cobalt waves. I had brought my oil pastels with me and, between outings, I sat in the living room with a cup of coffee and pieced together a beautiful scene of a sun rising over the shore. I slept more than usual, and it was a sound sleep. When it was time to leave, I felt rested.

Denial

July 2014

I hastened up the hill toward Hayward Street. I had been sitting in my office staring at the computer screen and hating myself for my inability to work. Coffee was a useless motivator. Sugar was useless as well. I was out of ideas, so I decided to go for a walk. Maybe if I walked far enough, the self-hatred would dissolve and I could actually get some work done. Anything.

Following the vacation in Charleston and the psychosis that came with it, the depression weighed heavier and heavier. I obsessively searched on the web to determine my prognosis. I had read dozens of abstracts on the National Institute for Mental Health's website. I had searched every combination of keywords. Bipolar disorder. Bipolar diagnosis. Bipolar psychosis. Psychosis. Psychotic features. Hallucinations. Delusions. Suicidal thoughts. Suicidal ideation. Bipolar and suicide. Most of the searches returned completely useless material, but occasionally I was able to find a tidbit of information that I found useful, which I noted in my journal. I had done the search several times before, and, for some reason, I expected a different result this time.

Frustrated with my inability to find what I needed—or at least what I wanted to hear—I asked Rachel point-blank what my diagnosis was. Granted, on that cold December day several months ago, Rachel told me I had bipolar disorder with psychotic features, but as I read about the illness, I learned that there were mainly two forms of bipolar disorder: bipolar I disorder and bipolar II disorder. Bipolar I disorder—the more severe of the two—required an episode of full-blown mania for diagnosis, and while I had teetered on some pretty high highs, I never experienced anything severe enough to require hospitalization, or so I thought. In fact, when I considered my experiences in terms of hospitalization, it seemed that my bipolar disorder was actually quite mild. After all, I had gone so long without treatment and was able to work despite most symptoms. But I needed the correct diagnosis. I needed the precision, the control that might not exist, so that I could project what the future might bring. My illness had been getting worse over the past several months, and I needed to know what exactly I was dealing with. What were the chances that I would attempt suicide? What were the chances that I would be hospitalized? And was recovery even possible?

Rachel, with her predictable honesty, explained to me this way: "Bipolar comes in many forms. Mild, moderate, severe, and severe with psychosis. You have severe bipolar with psychosis."

Severe bipolar with psychosis.

The words stung. When probed which type of bipolar disorder I had, she said, without hesitation, "Bipolar I."

I held no resentment towards Rachel, as she told me exactly

what I needed to know, which, in fact, was exactly what I had known all along. There was no more denying it. I was dealing with severe mental illness, and I needed to treat it as such. I was at a high risk for hospitalization and suicide, and I could now understand why Rachel was so concerned when I casually mentioned thoughts of self-harm or psychosis. While a diagnosis didn't change anything, it affected my perception of myself.

I'm crazy. I'm fucking crazy.

I was beating myself up as though I had some sort of control over it. I was doing all I was supposed to be doing: going to my appointments, reporting my symptoms as fully and honestly as I could to my psychiatrist and therapist, taking my medications as prescribed. Yet none of it seemed to help.

It had become common for me to put myself down. I was failing at my job. I was worthless at home. Susan and I argued nearly every day. I felt childish about how I relied on Rachel, calling her any and every time things started to get weird. I was a nuisance. A burden. The medications were worthless too. I was close to quitting altogether. On the Abilify, I had lost the ten pounds that I had put on, but the psychosis persisted; the weight loss was a moot point. Moreover, it was August and school would be starting in a few weeks. If I couldn't get a handle on my mental health, the coming semester would be completely hopeless, and that failure might cost me tenure.

My introspection made me angrier with myself. I walked furiously past the brick building housing my office and continued up the hill on a trail through the woods. For a brief moment, there within the shade of the trees, I felt peace. The wind rustled the branches and caressed my cheek with the last warmth of summer. The smell of earth and oak leaves took me back to nature, to that calm place I had found in Appalachia so long ago. I could hear cars and buses pass by noisily on the adjacent street, but I closed my eyes and imagined I was on a trail miles from civilization.

It was only a moment before I reached the edge of the woods. Instead of stopping or turning back, I continued along the road until the sidewalk ended. And then I kept going. The soft soil squished beneath my rigid dress shoes. I wished I could take them off and feel the cool grass against my bare feet. Or perhaps I could find a quiet spot in the sun and sprawl out on the ground. But I knew that I couldn't. It was a dangerous thing I was doing, aimlessly wandering so close to campus. Students or colleagues could see me. They would wonder what the hell I was doing.

Nevertheless, I continued along the road, which was lined by student housing on the left and woods on the right. I wished I could keep going; I wished the woods stretched forever, and I could walk the rocky terrain until my feet were sore and my legs could go no further. But I couldn't. I was at work. This was not a hike in the wilderness; it was a walk near campus. The walk of a delusional professor who was far too sick to work. *Severe bipolar with psychosis* is what Rachel called it. I needed to accept that I was seriously ill.

Angry that I had reached the student parking lot so quickly, I pulled out my phone to check the time. In total, I had walked for about half an hour. It was time to turn back on Hayward and walk the walk of shame—shame because I was unable to work, because I was wasting time, because I might lose my job, maybe my life, over this illness—back to my office. I inched my feet along, my pace slow as I tried to stretch out the last of the walk for as long as I could. I finally admitted defeat and entered the G.G. Brown building with its black-framed doors and ugly brown carpet. The halls were dark with yellowed paint on brick. I glanced at the massive industrial sketches of the construction of the Panama Canal lining the wall, which were done in charcoal on brown paper. As someone who had dabbled with charcoal, I was critical of the sketches. They were done in a rush and were far too sloppy. Plus, despite being a civil engineer myself, I had a strong dislike for the subject of the pictures. Cranes, concrete, steel—it was all so cold. I decided G.G. Brown was a prison. My prison. Concrete floors, thick masonry walls, exposed steel, and heavy wooden doors. Once locked inside, there was no way out. Adjacent to my office was the classroom in which I believed I had almost died at the hands of the weasel-faced boy. With the semester coming, I dreaded the thought of teaching again.

Thankful I did not encounter anyone in the hallway, I slipped into my office and closed the door silently behind me. I did not bother turning on the lights. I stood behind my desk, rolled the chair out of the way, and collapsed to the floor. I closed my eyes and lay there for two hours until I could rightfully clock out and go home. The only sounds were the insults that repeated over and over in my mind.

Tracing My Veins

August 2014

"What's going on with you? You're being kind of weird today."

I snickered. "What do you mean?" I responded, half-knowing I was not my usual self.

"I'm just getting an unusual vibe from you and thought you should know," Rachel said, her brow furrowed. She seemed to be growing impatient with me, as though I was a preschooler who refused to do as asked. She was scolding me, or at least that's what I thought, which made me feel both embarrassed and outraged. I did not like being talked down to.

"Okaaaaaay," I said in a strange, sarcastic tone and laughed with a hint of malice. I wanted to fight, not necessarily with Rachel, but with someone. My body was inhabited by some sort of evil creature that was intent on destroying everything in its path. Me, Rachel, the world. I wanted to throw away everything I owned and unleash the wickedness I had always held deep inside. I was not good or kind or compassionate; I was mean and spiteful. People had every right to steer clear of me. I was ugly, inside and out.

I knew I could act out with Rachel. I could start shouting or throwing things. She didn't care about me or anything that I had to say. She listened each week because it was her job. I was nothing more than a paycheck to her. She could walk out the door at the end of the day, go home, and never think about me again. Or, worse, she could judge me with her psychological nonsense. And I would continue to be the same pathetic loser I had always been, seeking attention by making something out of nothing. I was weak because I could not control my moods and behaviors. I was weak because I could not stop the supposed psychosis. I was weak because I had to rely on others to get me out of the mess I was in.

The fire had been growing inside me for days, and I was hell-bent on doing some damage. Experience told me I would eventually erupt, but I was able to keep my cool with Rachel. I somehow sensed the problem was with me, not her, and that it would be best if I just kept my mouth shut. Instead of giving in to the rage burning inside me, I looked away and changed the subject.

I left therapy feeling unsettled and sped back to work. I was overflowing with hatred. I hated my inability to work. I hated that I was blowing my opportunity as a professor at a world-class research university. I hated that I was a terrible wife and mother. I hated that I was unlikeable. I wanted to destroy myself, to sabotage my career and tear down the relationships I had built with Susan, with colleagues, with students, with anyone in my life. I wanted to self-destruct, to wipe my miserable existence from Earth. No one cared about me. No one wanted to be near me. These people in my life were false. The exchange with Rachel was merely the last straw, the final piece I needed to push me over the edge. By the time I reached my office, my blood boiled and my skin crawled.

Alone in my office with the door closed, I sat in the dark and stared, fixated, on my arms. The blood pulsed there, just beneath the surface. A force was drawing my attention to the veins protruding from my arms. Thick purple vessels raised from beneath my skin, twisting from my elbows to my fingertips, the threads that tenuously connected my body to me. I wanted to slice those perfect vessels and let the blood pour out, drain the life from my body.

Just do it.

My heart raced with the thought of death. It was the moment that separated suicidal ideation from suicide attempt. It was exhilarating, the feeling of life in the palms of my hands. One small move could end it all. Over the course of my life, I had learned how fragile life was, like a baby bird fallen from its nest.

Go on. Nobody thinks you can do it. You will show them.

I looked to the scissors on my desk. I pictured the struggle I would have, trying to saw my arms with the blunt edges of the scissors. "No," I whispered. "Scissors will not do the job."

I looked around my office for something sharper, and then I stopped. My body on the office floor covered in a pool of blood. What a horrible mess to leave behind. Who would find me? How long would it be before they came? What would initiate the search? Would the word get out that I was dead, that I had taken my own life? Would anyone bother to come to my funeral? And, moreover, how would Susan take the news? And Skye. Sweet Skye. Her hazel eyes and blonde hair.

A smile as wide as her face. The way she beamed at me when I walked into the room. "Mama! Mama!" her voice called out, full of innocence and unconditional love. The call of her voice brought tears to my eyes. I could not do that to Skye; it would destroy her. My job as a mother was to protect her, to shield her from harm and to keep her spirit high in the face of devastation. I could not do that if I was dead.

I decided to fight the compulsion to cut myself, but I could not keep from being obsessed with my veins. I could not stop my mind from fixating on the warm blood pumping from my heart to my fingertips and back again. I did not want to die, but I knew I could not live, at least not with this evil being inside of me. Instead of the scissors, I grabbed an ink pen and began tracing a vein on my left arm. I made a small, black mark before I stopped myself.

I'm at work. What will my colleagues think if they see me with ink all over my arms?

I retracted the tip of the pen and continued to trace the veins on my arms for several minutes. It was soothing but, as I regained consciousness, I became creeped out by my actions. I shook my head and snapped out of it. "It's getting too crazy in here," I said under my breath. I grabbed my keys and walked out of my office.

I was determined to walk as far as I needed to, to exhaust myself until the feeling passed. I hurried down Beal Avenue, past the Lurie Engineering Center and the Ford Presidential Library. Then I turned on Glazier Way and walked past the cemetery. I wanted to wander through the cemetery, to read the headstones and find the ones that were so ancient that the names had been eroded, the ones that were made of white stone and tinged green and brown. Those ones were best because they proved that nothing is permanent, that nature can and will destroy everything, even those markers identifying the bodies that had decomposed so long ago. But, worried someone would accuse me of trespassing, I stopped myself.

Instead, I continued down Glazier Way, and as I approached a line of cars at the stop sign, it dawned on me perhaps I should turn back. I made eye contact with the driver in one of the stopped cars—she scowled at me, making me feel uneasy. I quickened my pace, worrying someone I knew was surely in one of those cars. They would want to know why I was wandering, especially so far from my office. I turned at the stop sign and headed toward my office. Although I walked quickly, I tried to savor the beauty of the wildflowers in the median, but the noise from the traffic was too disruptive. I craved nature and was disturbed I could not find it on my walk.

I did not plan to return to work. After my two-mile hike, I stopped by my office merely to collect my backpack and then went directly to my van. Just being in my office gave me chills. Visions of tracing my arms flooded my mind. My office was no longer a place of safety, and I could not go back there until I could trust myself to be alone. I drove home, and as images of me cutting myself in my office raced through my head, I began to sob. *You will show them*, the voice had said. It was not me. I didn't want to kill myself; I wasn't the kind of person who would cut myself. Still, I had no control in the moment. I was losing my mind. And I almost tried to kill myself.

The next morning, I called Rachel and left her a voicemail.

"Hi Rachel, this is Ann Jeffers." I took a deep breath. "Firstly, I want to apologize for how I acted yesterday in therapy. I'm sorry for being uncooperative. You know that I am not usually confrontational. I wasn't myself." I paused and sniffled. "I'm not sure what was going on with me, but I want to apologize if I came off as mean." I took another deep breath and tried to steady my quivering voice. "Secondly, you had told me to call you if I was having thoughts of hurting myself. I wanted to let you know I almost cut myself yesterday." I sniffled again as I tried to suppress the tears. "I didn't though. I am safe now so you don't have to worry." I paused and then added, "You don't need to call me back."

It goes without saying that Rachel did call me back as soon as she received my message, not because it was her job, but because she really did care about me and wanted to make sure I was safe. Deep down, I knew that was true.

Back to Reality

August 2014

It took several days before I began to trust myself again. Having come so close to cutting, I needed to take all precautions to keep myself safe. At first, I avoided being alone. Knowing I could not yet return to my office, I spent my days at Starbucks, fueling up on caffeine and taking comfort in the noise of frothing milk. It was a busy place with people coming and going, ordering their iced double macchiatos with part skim, or whatever trendy four-dollar drinks were in season. I sat back with my black coffee and tried to focus. As I could not concentrate on work, I spent most of my time in reflection and journaling. I needed to figure out what was going on with me. Taking the last sip of my coffee, I sadly realized my mind was as empty as the paper cup before me.

I tried to move past the incident in my office, but I was overcome by the realization that my brain had been hijacked and programmed to kill me. A "command hallucination" is what Rachel had called it. The voice in my head told me to cut myself, but it was not motivated by thoughts or feelings that belonged to me. I grappled with the notion it may have been psychosis that had drawn me toward self-harm.

However, I was perplexed because a part of me believed there was some truth to that other version of me. How could I be sure that it was not really me wanting to take my life? What's more, I was embarrassed by my actions—the way that I behaved in Rachel's office and then went off to cut myself like some angst-ridden teenager. My brain echoed with my stupid, snickering voice in Rachel's office and my pathetic apology on her voicemail. I hated myself for it, and there was no way I could take it back.

A few days later, I wanted to surprise Susan with a home-cooked meal for dinner, so I stopped at the grocery store and picked up a bag of potatoes, a package of firm tofu, fresh bread, and green beans. I was beginning to feel more like myself, and it was time I ventured into the knife drawer—obviously, I could not go forever without cutting something.

Once we were home, Skye ran up the stairs to the couch where her tablet was charging, while I lugged the groceries to the kitchen.

As I unloaded the groceries and began setting up the kitchen, Skye called out, "Mama?"

"Yes, Skye?"

"I'm hungry."

"Dinner will be ready in a little bit. Do you want a snack?"

"Graham crackers," she said.

I reached in the pantry and handed her a stack of graham crackers before returning to the kitchen. The rough brown potatoes shone gold as I scrubbed them under water. I pulled out a cutting board, undid the childproof lock on the knife drawer, and slid it open. I winced at the sight of the blades. As I reached into the drawer and grabbed a large serrated knife, my hand shook at the feel of the steel tang and the look of the jagged teeth along the blade. I set the knife next to the cutting board, grabbed a potato, picked up the knife, sliced the potato carefully. My head was woozy with each movement of the knife, but my methodical action, which was necessary for providing dinner for my family, made it clear how absurd it was that I had almost tried to slit my wrists in my office.

The truth was I could not even watch my blood drawn at the doctor's office. In fact, I had never donated blood because the one time I tried, I nearly fainted when they pricked my finger to test my iron level. At a robust nineteen years of age, I was laid up in the Blood Mobile, sipping on apple juice and eating saltine crackers, not because I had heroically donated a pint of blood that would save someone's life, but because I could not get past a poke in the fingertip. I had no idea why I had become so obsessed with cutting myself. And now that I was feeling better, I was terrified of something I would never have the guts to do.

I finished slicing the potatoes, dumped them into the frying pan, and placed the knife in the sink, making sure the handle was facing up so that no one could get hurt. I didn't have to worry about cutting myself. In that moment, I was confident I was safe and could let down my guard.

The following day, I returned to my office to reclaim my space. Immediately, I grabbed the scissors from my desk and rushed to lock them away in the supply closet. I made sure there were no other objects I could harm myself with, and, after verifying the room was safe, propped my door open. I didn't like having my door open while I worked because I felt exposed like a fish in a bowl, but I had to make sure I would not do something stupid. Plus, I needed to work, and I tended to work my hardest when others were watching. I needed to stop doing weird and dangerous things, and, instead, I needed to focus on tenure.

I docked my laptop and opened a proposal I had barely begun working on. I needed funding, and the National Science Foundation had an upcoming submission deadline I was set on making. If I submitted on time, I would have a pending grant in my casebook, which might even be funded in time for the Executive Committee's review. I was in the home stretch for tenure, but I could not back down just yet. I needed one final push.

I opened the Word document, which had some section headings, a generic introductory figure, and a few random paragraphs. Over the next several hours, I began filling the canvas with paint, adding subheadings and figures, and deepening the narrative. I searched the web for references to back up my methodology, and soon my proposal was turning into an authentic scientific argument. I continued to work through the afternoon, and it was not long before it was time to pack up and head home. As I locked up my office, I breathed easily, even with a sense of pride.

Despite my smooth recovery, a ghost haunted me on the way home. The ghost that drew me to almost taking my life. In the car, my mind raced with the images of death that had recently overpowered me. I shuddered at thoughts of knives and pills and leaps from high places. It wasn't me, but I was weak to resist it.

A few days later, I had yet another appointment with Dr. Park. After hearing about the events that had unraveled over the past few weeks, she switched my antipsychotic medication yet again, this time to Risperdal. She said this was a drug that was a bit more potent than the previous ones, one that was more of a go-to medication for psychotic disorders. As I accepted the prescription, I tried to catch my breath and push back the sense of doom. Things were getting worse, and there was no turning back.

Another Reality

August 2014

It was bedtime, and I teemed with energy. It was Susan's night to put Skye to bed, so I made my way to the master bedroom. I had been monitoring my moods and sleep in a very scientific manner over the past several months, and my mood chart clearly showed I was becoming manic. There was nothing I could do except sit back and enjoy the ride. Undoubtedly, psychosis was coming on—I had begun to hear the telltale static and whispering. My thoughts wandered off-course, becoming more bizarre, and I was unnecessarily jumpy as though dangers might appear in places I otherwise considered safe.

As I lay in bed, the hallway light shone on my arm, giving my skin the appearance of the bark of a wild cherry tree. The surface of my arm was purplish black with flecks of white formed by what was presumably salt crusted on my skin from the warm summer day. I twisted my arm in the light to savor its beauty. My arm did not feel real. My body was not real either. I began to question whether anything was real. I inspected my limb as though it was a twig I had found lying in the grass. It held the beauty and mystery and wonder of nature. *If only I could capture it—*

Susan came into the room to grab her glasses. "Are you okay?" she asked as she observed me twisting my arm in the light.

"Oh," I said, jumping at the realization she was watching me. "I'm fine. Just a little tired."

"Are you going to tell me goodnight?" She was put off by the fact that I had climbed in bed before Skye was even asleep. Her tone made it clear she wasn't happy with me.

"Yeah, of course." I was pretending not to be hurt by her harsh approach. I mustered all the sweetness I could fake and gave her my best attempt at a smile. "Goodnight, lady."

She leaned in gently and gave me a kiss. I was left alone in darkness to fight my way to sleep.

My body was buzzing. My mind followed the hum of the air conditioner, and within minutes, a somber tune emanated from the wall behind my head. It was a sweet, melancholic melody played on an acoustic piano. It evoked the emotion of Beethoven's *Moonlight Sonata*, but this piece was far more modern.

Perhaps I could record the tune somehow, transcribe it on paper—

I stopped myself. While I had studied piano as a child, I lacked the skill of writing sheet music. The minute I grabbed a sheet of paper, the music would be gone, leaving me disappointed. Instead, I stretched my body out, placing my left arm behind my head, and I savored the sweet melody while it lasted. As I listened, my head swayed gently from side to side.

This isn't real.

I squeezed my eyes tight and pulled the covers over my head, hoping the music would cease. Despite its beauty, this music was merely a symptom of my psychosis. Even worse, I couldn't share the beauty of this experience with others. The music was breathtaking, and yet it would fall on my ears only. What a precious waste.

Go to sleep, Ann.

I rolled to my side, the melody soothing me to sleep.

The following day, with my schedule completely open aside from a meeting with my research group, I planned to work from home. I took every opportunity to work from home, mostly because the building I worked in brought up dreadful thoughts of school shootings and suicide. In addition, I could spare myself the trouble of dressing respectably and lay around in my pajamas all day. The house was empty, with Susan at work and Skye at daycare, meaning I was free to lounge wherever without disruption. "Work from home," though, was merely a phrase built with good intentions. The only truth to it was that I stayed home—I stayed home and avoided anything having to do with work. I spent hours unaccountable, searching the web, laying on the couch, or staring at the maple tree outside my front window. On the rare occasion I had energy, I might do a repair on the house or run an errand. Most days were a waste, and this particular Friday was lost in Wasteland, that is, until the alarm went off on my phone, signifying that the meeting with my students started in ten minutes.

"Shit!" I yelled to an empty house, realizing I would be late for the meeting due to the thirty-minute commute. Without time to shower, I dusted my hair to the side and hurried to campus. Once there, I circled the student lot in search of a parking spot, finally eyeing the only open one, far in the back corner of the lot. I stomped on the gas pedal so as not to lose the spot to one of the several other cars lurking nearby. The frantic haze in my head had not faded, and I worried about how I might come across to my students, who, as far as I could tell, knew nothing of my illness.

I climbed down the hill to the sidewalk and rushed toward my office. Thoughts raced through my head lightly and quickly, like the chatter of a squirrel. The sun beamed bright and warm, giving the world a blueish hue. As I walked, my eyes darted back and forth between each and every pockmark in the concrete sidewalk.

A bee! My eye caught a large insect on the sidewalk. We were in the dog days of summer. Bees were common this time of year. I walked on.

Another bee. Then, I saw another and yet another. The fourth bee looked different. Its body was long and deformed. Unlike most bees I had seen, this one was large, wiry, and had white stripes. I thought back to the bees I had seen previously. Were these bees of the same species, or had they begun morphing shape like some alien form of insect? A few more crawled along the cement, each wirier and more deformed than the last. Panic burst through my chest.

Wait. Is this real?

It dawned on me that this unusual sighting of bees was occurring just after a night in which I lulled myself to sleep with music coming from my walls. My mind was racing. The world was unreal. I wasn't sleeping. I was manic.

Okay. The next bee that I see, I will stop and pretend to tie my shoe. That way, I can get down and take a closer look.

And just as I was about to kneel down to pretend to tie my leather dress shoes, the bees were entirely gone.

Because I was running late for my meeting, I continued on. Part of me wanted to turn back so I could see the cluster of bees I had just walked over, but part of me was scared. I didn't know what I would do if I turned around and there were no bees—no bees, meaning my mind had made up the whole thing. No more bees appeared on my walk, but I kept scanning the sidewalk frantically, searching for any sign of bees. The absence of bees cranked up the clutching panic.

In the conference room, five students sat around the table, ready to begin the discussion. I was sweating and out of breath, my hair greasy from not taking a shower.

Be normal.

"Sorry I'm running a little late," I said to the group. And then I lied, "I'm coming from an off-campus appointment that ran over."

"It's okay, Dr. Jeffers," Blake said in his usual, cheery manner, and the other students nodded in agreement.

"Alright, so let's get started," I said in the tone of a professor who had it together.

The students followed by taking turns giving short presentations on their research. I did my best to stay focused and to engage in discussion when needed. I asked thoughtful questions following each presentation, and I got a sense the students would walk away from the meeting with fresh ideas, per usual. It was an unusual feeling to be able to focus on work while facing fears in the back of my mind that I was completely losing it. I dreaded the end of the meeting because I would be forced to trace my path back to the parking lot and face the bees, whether they were real or not.

The meeting ended without incident, and as I exited the building, I was blasted by the August heat. The sun blazed, and sweat dripped down my forehead almost immediately. I walked slowly toward the parking lot, my eyes scanning every mark on the sidewalk. It was not long before I reached the point where I had seen the bees. I took a deep breath.

If the bees were real, then surely I will see at least one of them again.

I slowed my pace further and searched every crack and crevice in the pavement. Thinking maybe a breeze had blown the bees away, I scoured the edge of the sidewalk lining the grass. No bees there, so I stepped into the road when no cars were coming and inspected the curb, the drains, and even the road, all the way to the median. Eventually, I returned to the sidewalk and made it to the hill leading to my parking spot. As the realization hit me that the bees were not real, tears burned in the corners of my eyes. No bees—not a sliver of evidence of their existence.

I spent the rest of the afternoon analyzing what had happened. I wrote the following in my journal:

"I saw bees. The bees changed shape. When I questioned whether it was a hallucination and planned to look more closely, I immediately stopped seeing bees. I have never seen bees like that before. I did not go back immediately to check if the bees were still there, but I did return an hour later and the bees were gone. They were not on the sidewalk, not in the grass, and not in the road. What's more, I have been a little manic and not sleeping well, and I just started a new antipsychotic medication."

As I objectively wrote down the facts, it became apparent that I had most likely had a visual hallucination, one that was more realistic than any of my prior hallucinations. It took me a day before I mustered the courage to call Dr. Park. By that point, I had analyzed the scenario over and over until my head hurt and my heart wanted to explode. I had not slept, and I was convinced I was certifiably crazy.

The following morning, I left a message on Dr. Park's voicemail. She called me back quickly and increased my dose of Risperdal. We had reached the therapeutic level of Lamictal, my mood stabilizer, although I wondered if it did anything to stabilize my mood given the cycles of mania and depression I was experiencing. I braced myself for the side effects that came with a med adjustment and prayed the increase in Risperdal would curb the psychosis.

Therapy (Part 4)

August 2014

I sunk into the oversized couch in Rachel's office. Across from me hung a wicker wreath decorated with ribbon and beads that was clearly homemade. Not in a tacky Martha Stewart way, but rather in a way that suggested the person who made it took great pleasure in combining handfuls of sparkly junk from Joann Fabrics and creating something uniquely appealing. The wreath added some warmth to her otherwise depressing office. Indeed, Rachel had made a few other small changes to make the place more homelike. Flowers on the coffee table. A new clock above the desk. *Not bad*, I thought.

"So, what's going on?" she asked in her usual manner. She took a sip of her oversized iced tea.

"Well, the other night, I heard music in my bedroom again." I paused, allowing Rachel to nod her head thoughtfully. "And on Friday I was walking over bees, but I'm pretty sure they weren't really there."

"Why do you think they weren't real?" she asked. She set her cup down on her desk and turned to face me.

"Okay, well, I know *bees* are real. But these ones were different."

"How so?"

I explained how I had seen the bees lining the sidewalk, one after another, and how I had devised a plan to pretend to tie my shoe when the bees disappeared.

Rachel furrowed her brow. "Hmm. Interesting. So how were these bees different?"

"Ah, well!" I slapped my knee for emphasis. "They had *white* stripes. All the bees I have seen in my life have had yellow stripes, not white. I did find one type of bee—a bald-faced hornet—that does have white stripes, and it is native to Michigan. But the image that came up in my Google search looked nothing like the bees that I saw."

"Okay." She spoke slowly, cautiously.

"And my bees were wiry." I added, "And I'm pretty sure they changed shape. And why did they disappear when I decided to take a closer look?"

"Those are all very good points," she said, validating my thought process.

I took a deep breath. "They aren't real, are they?"

Rachel weighed the evidence for a moment, and then said, "It's hard to say. I mean, there are bees in Michigan. I'm not sure about bees with white stripes though."

"I know, right? It's like one day I'm hearing music and the next I'm seeing bees!" My voice had gotten louder, and an exaggerated smile had formed across my face. I could feel my cheek muscles flex as I talked. "And I was like, 'Here's one bee, and another, and another, and another!' Then, when I finally get the idea to look at them more closely—poof! They're gone!" I let out a heavy, exaggerated laugh. "It's ridiculous!"

Rachel studied me, frowning. Finally, she asked, "Why are you laughing?"

"Because it's funny!" I insisted.

"What's funny?" Rachel was wholly unamused. It was as though I was the teenager who had come home in the middle of the night from a party at a friend's house, and Rachel was the mom who saw right through my marijuana-laced lies.

"Bees are funny!" I shouted, and I let out an uncharacteristic laugh.

"Explain what you mean, because I don't think bees are funny." Rachel was dead serious. She did not see humor in any of it.

"I mean, I came up with this grand plan to stop and pretend to tie my shoes." Realizing Rachel was not finding it amusing, I spelled it out for her. "My shoes didn't even have laces! I was *wearing* shoes that *didn't* have laces! And I didn't want to look like an idiot, searching the ground for bees. Like people would know what I was doing! And as if I care what people think, anyway!"

"I don't think it's funny," she said with a stone-cold face.

"Come on! It's hilarious," I said loudly and slapped my knee as if I had just dropped the punchline to a very funny joke. However, I began to feel my face burn in embarrassment. She was on to me.

"Well, I don't think it's funny at all," Rachel maintained.

"It has to be funny," I said forcefully. The smile dropped from my face and my tone darkened, my words pressed through clenched teeth. "It *has* to be funny. Because if it's not funny—"

My eyes filled with tears.

"—then it's really *fucking* scary."

A tear rolled down my cheek, and Rachel handed me the box of tissues. I blew my nose and stuffed the wad of wet tissue into my pants pocket.

"I know," Rachel said, the empathy now apparent.

"I told Dr. Park," I said more quietly. "She increased the Risperdal. It's not going to work. Nothing is going to work."

"I know it's frustrating. It can take a long time to find a cocktail that works."

I sighed. "I've been trying for *months*, and I'm not getting any better."

"You are doing everything right. And Dr. Park knows what she's doing. Unfortunately, there is a lot of trial and error involved with psychiatric medicine. That's just how it is. Please try to be patient."

I looked down at the floor in resignation. "I'm not optimistic this is going to work."

"I know, hon. Try to hang in there."

Running Away

August 2014

"Go to work," I said through clenched teeth as I clutched the steering wheel. It was the end of August, my last opportunity before classes started and life became busy again. I had a ton of work to do, but I sat in the student parking lot unable to even open the van door, let alone go to my office. I was motionless, a monolith of stone, and despite all my willpower, I was unable to move.

"Fuck it," I shouted, as my hands came down hard on the steering wheel. I turned the key in the ignition and backed out of my parking space. Speeding, I merged onto the highway, and then I pressed down on the gas pedal until my van reached eighty miles per hour. I did not care that I was going faster than I normally would. I did not care that I was putting my life in danger.

Go. Just go.

I pushed down further on the accelerator and weaved past the vehicles that had slowed to exit or enter the highway.

Keep going. Until the plains turn to mountains, and the mountains turn to sandy beaches.

I had visions of running, like the running I did when I

lived in Virginia. I wanted to drive away from my problems. I craved the release the beach gave me in the months following the Virginia Tech shooting. No matter how wrecked I was, the warm ocean waves could restore me into something that resembled me.

When you reach the beach, keep going. Until the ocean swallows you whole. Make up a new name. Come up with a new look. Lose your family. Find something mindless and laborious to do, like serve food at a restaurant or start a landscaping business. Something you are good at. Something that does not care if you are psychotic. Bees. Demons. Voices. Music. Just go. And keep going.

The highway signs told me I was getting closer to home. A voice of reason spoke up, softly and sweetly.

Stop. You can't run. You need to go home, Ann. You are not well.

Feeling torn between running to freedom and steering safely toward home, I hit the brakes and veered off the exit. I headed in the direction of my home, but I was still compelled to keep driving. I thought about where the road would take me if I kept going past my house. I was headed westward—Indiana cornfields.

There is more beyond the cornfields.

Mountains, rivers, trails, and wildlife. I dreamed of nature, of birds singing their carefree songs and of wind-waving leaves. I thought back to the trip that my parents took my brothers and me on before we moved to Germany. We had visited nearly all the National Parks in Colorado and Utah. The world was so much larger and beautiful in the West among the massive mountains and the steep canyons, the endless red rock.

As I drove on, the sky opened up, releasing a ray of sunlight that blinded me. Even though my vision temporarily blackened, I added pressure to the gas pedal and tightened my hold on the steering wheel.

Nothing will stop me. I will become a new me—a somebody. There will be no more pain. No more failure. No one holding me back.

I blinked and regained my vision just in time to avoid rear-ending a delivery truck. I drove through a few more lights until I reached the downtown traffic light in the city where I lived. Instead of turning toward my house, I kept going, but instantly felt regret. My gaze darted left and right for some sort of sign as to what I should do. Then I saw a sign for a park.

Stop. Think out a plan.

If I ran away, it would be for good. I was walking away from my job and quite possibly my family. It seemed like a decision that should have some thought put into it first. I pulled into the parking lot at the park, grabbed my journal, and found a picnic table in the shade.

Even though it was mid-morning, the heat rose up from the pavement and settled in the air. It pained me to think that I was in the midst of summer and yet my mood was so dreadful. My skin was crawling, and it seemed running was the only way to make it stop. My mind buzzed with ideas. Ideas of running. Ideas of where I could go. Ideas of starting over. Ideas of life without a family. I thought about how easy it would be to start over. I already had so much experience, not just in my academic career path but also in my previous dead-end jobs. I had served food, sold cutlery, lifeguarded, worked in construction. These were all skills that would take me far in this new life I envisioned.

Maybe you should bounce this idea off Rachel first.

Rachel was my sounding board, and if something in my plans did not make sense, she would set me straight. I picked up my phone and dialed her voicemail. After listening to her greeting, I hung up.

She is on vacation. Why would I bother her like that? And what would I even say to her?

A car pulled into the lot. I feared whoever was inside was going to report my absence to the university, as though my work took attendance. Heck, they didn't even pay me to work during the summers. Two men in their forties got out of the car. I gripped my journal tightly but relaxed as they walked toward the pavilion. I opened my journal to a blank page. As I had done so many times when I feared what to say on the phone, I began writing a script for myself:

> "Hi Rachel, this is Ann Jeffers. I know you are on vacation, and I'm sorry to bother you. I want to give you a heads-up that things have not been good with me. The hallucinations and paranoia have become more frequent, and I very nearly cut myself last week. I just want to let you know. You don't need to call me back. I have an appointment with Dr. Park this afternoon."

I paused and then added, "Also, I'm afraid I am trying to sabotage my career as a form of self-harm." Then, feeling like that was a strange way to end a voicemail, I finished with, "I'll talk to you next week." I might have been at the point of leaving my family, but I was not about to cancel an appointment. I would be at my appointment with Rachel, punctual as ever, regardless of whether I had walked away from all I held sacred in my life.

Certain I had put together the right things to say, I picked up my phone again and dialed Rachel's voicemail. I listened to her greeting again, but I could not bring myself to talk. I hung up before the beep. Something about the line of self-sabotage made my planned speech seem unusual to me.

Back and forth, I reviewed my script. I needed to tell Rachel I was not well, but something about the process was all wrong. I picked up my phone a third time, dialed Rachel's number—but hung up before entering her extension.

"Stupid!"

I hit my head with my hand, and then glanced around to see if someone was watching me.

I was getting nowhere dialing Rachel's number and continuously hanging up. Calling Rachel was a bad idea. Running away was a bad idea. Feeling embarrassed by my actions, I got up and walked back to my car.

The Weight of Depression

August 2014

Despite the shining afternoon sun, I donned a cloak made of lead. It slowed my movements and covered me in darkness, its opaque surface preventing any light from illuminating my world within. It wasn't long before the weight of the cloak dragged me to the floor. As my body slid from my chair, I scrambled to reach for something to hold onto. My red Columbia fleece. I balled it up under my head, a pillow to break my descent to the cold concrete. I closed my eyes and breathed slowly, but I could not sleep. I wanted to sleep. I *needed* to sleep. If only I could wash away the sickness. A drink of cold water, a breath of fresh air, a much-needed slumber, *anything* to bring life to my wasted body. But instead, I lay on the floor of my office, door locked, lights dimmed, praying that no one would disturb my rest.

The buses growled with their coming and going from the bus stop outside my window. The noise was relentless. The sounds that came from the fabrication shop below—the "clank," "bang," and "zhreeee"—were unsettling. It was as if the circular saw buzzed through my stillness and the hammer shattered my quietude.

If only I could have slept.

If. Only. I. Could. Have. Slept.

Snap out of it.

The cardinal outside my window taunted me with his incessant chirping. His cheerfulness tormented me as if to say, "Look how unalive you are, you pathetic, miserable soul." With his bright coat of feathers and his quick tilt of the head, he pecked at the window curiously.

Disgusted, I rolled away from the window to face the underside of my desk. The desk was worn from its decades of service. Its metal was chipped and bent in various places, and its beige paint was smattered with brown stains and sticky outlines of masking tape that had randomly been applied on its surfaces. The desk reminded me of myself. Pathetic. Lifeless. No longer needed.

Get up.

But I could not rise. My pleas were hopeless. Every ounce of strength had been sucked from my veins. All that was left was the carcass on the floor of my office. I could already smell the meat beginning to rot. I waited patiently for the vultures to come and pick at my fragile remains. It would not be long before I would decompose to a fine powder that would be swept away in a gentle and lively breeze.

This must be what death feels like.

No, death would've been better than this. Better than suffering through such a dreadful existence.

I pondered death but decided the energy required to devise a plan and carry it out was beyond my ability in my crippled state. Instead, I sighed and rolled back toward the window.

The ghastly cardinal had flown away, leaving a peaceful scene before me. The pines swayed in the breeze, causing the light to glisten in my eyes. I lusted for the sun, whose golden rays beckoned like the Lorelei, the fabled woman whose beauty and song drew the attention of sailors, causing their ships to crash into the rocks. I felt my body lifting from the floor, my arms stretched toward the sun, my mind so numb that it was incapable of feeling my skin scorching as I neared the sun's surface. Burnt hair, melted skin. When I pulled my hands back, there was nothing but charcoal for my appendages. The burns left a blackness that perfectly matched the blackness of my mind and heart.

As I fantasized about being destroyed by the sun, I realized that I dreamt of something more than death—a death that was deader than death—because it was the only way to stop the sickening feeling that plagued my body and mind. I could not see my family. I could not see life. Death was the only way. And because I couldn't die *enough*, I needed to sleep. If I could sleep, I at least knew that someday—maybe not tomorrow, maybe not next week, but someday—my mood would change, and I would be able to see the world in color again.

Hold on, Ann. Go to sleep.

I closed my eyes, breathed deeply, and prayed for time to pass.

A Brief Conversation with Susan

August 2014

The door opened, and Susan entered the house. She lay her things on the couch, went to the kitchen to wash her hands, and then came into the living room, where I lay on the loveseat. Skye had her tablet and was playing a game. I stared at the floor, analyzing the patterns in the carpet.

"Hey," Susan said.

"Hey." I didn't look up.

"How was work?"

"Fine," I lied.

"Anything happen?"

"No. Just trying to finish this proposal before school starts." I hadn't touched the proposal in weeks.

"How was Skye's day?"

"Good." Sensing my one-word answers were not sufficient, I said, "The daycare got a new playhouse for the kids. Skye really enjoys the kitchen area. She was baking cookies today."

Hearing her name, Skye looked up from her tablet and smiled at me. I smiled back, although I could tell my face looked worn. I didn't know the last time I had had a good night's sleep, and crying was something I did pretty much daily.

Without moving, my eyes met Susan's. "How was your day?"

Her response was nothing but ordinary. She talked about her day at work, sharing story after story of her interactions with coworkers and students on campus. They were busy already with the return of students for the fall. Thankfully, Susan was a talker. She could talk and talk without needing much input from me. So while I was woefully depressed and had even thought about running away, it was fairly easy for me to pretend everything was normal.

It had become regular practice for me to keep my mental illness to myself. Susan didn't understand the psychosis, and there wasn't much benefit to telling her about it anyway. I never felt comforted telling her about my hallucinations—speaking the words aloud to her and observing her eyes widen just made me feel crazy—and there was nothing she could do to make the psychosis stop. I brought this up to Rachel, and she suggested maybe I didn't need to tell Susan everything. It seemed disingenuous, but I was willing to give it a try.

So when I thought about cutting myself, I said nothing to Susan. And when I saw the bees and heard the music from my walls, I said nothing to Susan. And when I thought about running away for an afternoon, I said nothing to Susan. And when I lay on the floor of my office having visions of death, I said nothing to Susan. Mental illness was *my* battle. Instead,

I pretended that everything was normal, that I went to my office every day, worked on my work, and shuttled Skye to and from daycare. Everything was *fine*—at least that is the story I conveyed to my wife.

Calling Home

August 2014

"Hello?"

"Hey, Mom," I said into the phone. "How's it going?"

"Oh, I was just getting ready to wash the siding with the pressure washer. The outside of this house is so filthy from that damn maple tree." She took a moment to catch her breath and then muttered, "I'm so glad your dad had it cut down."

"Yeah," I said passively, not wanting to change the subject abruptly. While I normally checked in with my parents once a week, this time I had a purpose for calling. However, I always felt like a kid when I talked to my parents, so I listened for several minutes while my mom told me how wonderful her pressure washer was. She then turned the conversation to me.

"So what's up?" she asked.

"Things are going well here," I lied, and then I made up all sorts of nonsense about how great things were at work. I stopped myself midway through and sheepishly confided, "I'm still trying to get this bipolar thing under control."

"How are you feeling?"

"I'm good. I mean, my moods are all over the map, but the medications are helping."

"Well, that's good," she said.

"It's the symptoms of psychosis that are bothering me. We haven't been able to find the right antipsychotic medication."

"Oh yeah?" she said.

I could tell my mental health was a subject that made my parents uncomfortable. They never asked about it unless I brought it up first, which made me feel uncomfortable sharing my experience with them. It was not that they didn't care; I believe it had more to do with the fact that it was something so foreign to them. Just as I was terrified of the term "psychosis," surely they too battled the stigma of my illness. I mean, who wants to come to grips with their daughter having bipolar disorder with psychotic features? The truth is that parents have only limited control over how their children turn out, but any good parent will wonder if they are the cause of their child's flaws.

"I was wondering if you could tell me about the time Grandpap was hospitalized."

"Oh, okay," she said with a little hesitation. I had caught her off-guard with my question, but I knew she would have no trouble providing an answer.

My grandfather was a World War II veteran. He was assigned to an aircraft carrier—the U.S.S. Princeton—which patrolled the Asian Pacific at the height of the war. The Princeton went under attack in October 1944 and was sunk by bombs dropped by Japanese fighter planes. A hundred of his shipmates were killed in the attack, and many more sailors died during the battle. My grandfather was rescued by a neighboring ship, and he returned to the U.S. mostly unharmed, physically.

However, his service left deep emotional scars that never fully healed. He took to drinking and lived a wild life working for the railroad. When I thought of my grandfather—at least the man he was before he had his stroke—I pictured a jovial man with a can of Old Milwaukee's Best in his hand, telling outrageous stories from his time on the railroad or singing clips from old country songs. However, my mom once disclosed to me a darker side to his drinking from her childhood, the side in which my grandfather, who was a few beers in, would pull my mom and her younger brother under his arms and tell them stories from the time the Princeton was sunk—stories of explosions and great fires and bodies floating in the frigid ocean.

He told these horrific stories to two children who could make no sense, who were frightened by seeing their father break down in a drunken and blubbering mess, and who, as small children, were powerless to stop it. Decades later, when I came into the picture, my mom's family celebrated my grandfather as a hero for his service. After my mom painted that picture of her father for me, I no longer saw him as a war hero; I saw a man who had been broken by war.

It was not the PTSD or alcohol abuse that I needed answers on though. I wanted to know about his recent psychotic episode. A few years prior to my diagnosis of bipolar disorder, my grandfather—who was in his late eighties—had awoken one morning convinced he had caught my grandmother having sex with another man in the kitchen in the middle of the night. It did not matter that Grandma, who needed a cane to get around, lacked the physical capacity to actually get down to, let alone get up from, the kitchen floor. He saw it with his own two eyes though, and no amount of logic could change his thinking. Following the alleged incident, he persistently accused my grandmother until he threatened to harm either himself or my grandmother, at which point he was "voluntarily" admitted to the psych ward. They ruled out dementia—in fact, his mind was sharp as a tack, aside from that one persistent delusion. He was prescribed an antipsychotic medication, and he eventually came out of it. Following his release, he would periodically bring the incident up and accuse my grandmother of being unfaithful, and for the years to follow, my mom insisted he was not well.

My mom told me once again about the night that Grandpap was hospitalized. Hearing it a second time helped me make sense of the event, but I wanted to know more.

It seemed odd to me that a person would have a psychotic episode randomly and so late in life. There had to be more to the story. "What about before that? Did he ever show signs of mental illness before that?"

"Honestly, I think there has always been something going on," she said, and then she explained how her parents argued when my mom was growing up. "He was always accusing her of things that were untrue. They used to go back in the bedroom and have these awful arguments. I never knew what it was about. He never sought help for any of it though, and, as far as I know, he never received any sort of diagnosis." She paused and then said, "But it was a different time. We didn't talk about those kinds of things back then."

I let out a sigh. I would not be able to get what I wanted: a documented mental health history of my grandfather. The truth was his behaviors were not documented and, in fact, the family kept it under the rug until he eventually had to be hospitalized.

There was a brief pause, and then she said, "I sometimes see things too." My heart skipped a beat. She continued, "Like, I will be sitting in the living room and see a shadow out of the corner of my eye that looks like a mouse. It usually only happens when I'm really tired though. Maybe that is what is going on with you."

Unsure of where she was going with the conversation, I said, "Mom, I think everybody sees things in the corner of their eyes. It's very different when you hear voices though. I can't deny the voices that say very specific words to me."

"No, I guess you are right."

"And seeing a demon or a dead person is very different from a shadow in the corner of my eye. In fact the other day, I was seeing bees that I'm pretty sure were not real." I understood my mom probably did not want to accept my psychosis any more than I wanted to, but I was starting to get a little irritated that she was downplaying my symptoms into something that would otherwise be considered an everyday occurrence. "It was very scary."

"Oh my!"

Realizing I may have overshared, I said, "I mean, my doctor adjusted my medication and I'm better now. But, yeah, it was kind of scary at the time."

"I guess you are right. Seeing a shadow and thinking it is a mouse is different." She paused. "The medication is working though, right?"

I lied. "Oh, yeah, I'm doing much better with it. It's just taking us some time to fine-tune everything."

"That's so great to hear. Well, if you ever need to talk—"

"Thanks, Mom. But really, I'll be fine."

I stepped out on the deck connected to the kitchen and looked out over the field lining the back of our property. The sun warmed my cheeks. A noisy blue jay landed in a tree next to the house, reminding me that it was about time to pick up Skye from daycare.

Teaching with Visions of Death

September 2014

Behind my desk, I watched the clock on the computer screen jump one minute ahead, sending a dagger through my chest. My heart beat fast, and my palms were on fire. I wished for the courage to cancel class because I was certain the shooter would emerge today. Nevertheless, I remained motionless with my eyes fixed on the clock, unable to gather my notes—and my ideas—about the material I needed to cover in lecture. Fortunately, I had gotten more comfortable with winging it over my years of teaching. It was as though someone could hand me notes on any topic, and I could step in front of the classroom and begin reciting the content with ease, mixing theoretical concepts and equations on the board with spontaneous narrative for context. I was becoming an expert of many things, and my experience helped guide the words as I taught.

The classroom was directly outside my office, which added to my anxiety. While I kept my office door closed, I could hear the students shuffling into the room and dropping their backpacks on the tables. The room brightened with chatter about homework and projects. We were a few weeks into the semester already, and while I normally had gotten to know many of the students in my classes by this point, my anxiety had formed a barrier, blocking my view of faces during the lecture. I was so set on surviving each day that I failed to connect with my students in any meaningful way. Instead, I averted my eyes when I turned toward the class, feeling only the presence of the weasel-faced boy who might come in at any moment.

I waited until exactly two minutes before the start of class and then collected my notes, put my cell phone in my back pocket, and grabbed my keys from the desk. There was a time when I left my cell phone back in my office for fear of the disruption, but these days I kept it on me, realizing I needed to be able to call 9-1-1 when the shooter appeared. Balancing my keys and notebook in my left hand, I flipped the office light off and pulled the door closed with my right. I took a deep breath and stepped into the classroom, my eyes awkwardly fixed on the brown carpet. I lay my things on the table at the front of the room, and then I stepped onto the stage. The class continued their talking while I pulled a few sheets of paper from my notebook. With my back to the class, I wrote some notes on the chalkboard to summarize the material covered in the previous lecture. I was teaching a graduate class on finite element analysis, which was a computational method used in solid mechanics, among other fields. There were more than forty students enrolled in the class, and many were from departments other than my own.

"Okay, let's go ahead and get started," I called out once I had finished writing the notes on the board. After a moment, the room quieted, and I was able to begin my review of the prior class. "We have been discussing the isoparametric formulation, and in class last time, we derived the equations for the four-node quadrilateral element," I said, continuing to look at the ground. "Today, we will talk about numerical integration and how it can be used to carry out the integration needed to compute the stiffness matrix within a computer code. You will recall from last time that the Jacobian is not constant for a distorted element, and therefore we cannot do the integration analytically. You have probably seen a little bit of numerical integration in other classes that you have taken. How many of you have seen something like the trapezoid rule before?" I asked, knowing I would need to make eye contact with the class. I scanned the room, where hands were raised in reluctant, bored participation. I looked for the weasel-faced boy, but he was not there.

An image flashed in my mind: a classroom soaked in a pool of blood. The bodies of students fallen over tables and chairs, marked by gunshot wounds that bled profusely. Some students, still alive, wailed in pain.

"Good," I said, maintaining the tone of a professor despite the gory scene I had just witnessed. "Well, today we are going to talk about an integration technique called Gauss quadrature." I turned to the board and began writing some notes while giving an explanation. I tried to keep my hands steady as I wrote, even though I thought I might pass out. I worked on the board for several minutes, and my confidence grew the more I focused on the mathematical technique I was teaching. There was something about the familiarity of Gauss quadrature that calmed me.

Where is that echo coming from? It seems if I stand exactly at the middle of the board, I can hear my voice echo, like there is cavity above me. What if someone is listening to me? I don't see an opening though.

All eyes on me, boring into me, burning. Because I was talking about one thing and thinking another, the words tumbled out, mixed up, without my knowing. I flipped forward in my notes to an example.

"Let's look at the integration of a polynomial, for which we have an exact solution. I want you to solve the problem using one-point and two-point Gauss quadrature and compare to the exact solution. Take a few minutes to work on this, and then we will come together to see what you have come up with."

I rushed out of the classroom and down the hallway. I took a few sips of the cool water from the water fountain and attempted to center myself. Counting my breaths, I returned to the classroom to find most students working diligently on the task I had assigned. *Safe so far.*

I allowed the students to work for a few more minutes, and as they worked, I tried to study their faces. They were all so foreign to me. I felt bad I was still so disconnected at this point in the semester; teaching had become such a struggle.

"Okay, let's see what you have come up with," I said, and I solicited answers from the class. After talking through the solution, I moved on to the next topic. In my usual form, I wrote on the board while I talked, keeping my back to the class. Even though I had recovered some during the short break, I remained on edge.

I was mid-sentence when I saw a man outside the classroom door. My mind flashed again. This time, he entered the room and began shooting. I saw the bodies of students fall, many more scattered to exit the room. I stood helpless at the front of the classroom as the horrid scene played out before me. There were screams. So much blood. I couldn't stop it. There was nothing I could do.

Still, I continued teaching. I stuttered a moment, choking on the words I could no longer force out. I looked for the fastest way to wrap up the class without letting on that I was about to have a panic attack.

"Sorry, my words got a little tripped up," I said and let out a nervous laugh. "Since we are just about out of time, I think we should go ahead and stop here. Next class, we will talk about isoparametric triangular elements."

I snatched up my notebook and keys from the front table and darted across the hall to my office without giving any of the students a chance to ask questions.

The Airport

November 2014

I wandered through the terminal in search of something, unsure what. All airports were the same. Harsh fluorescent lights, stale air, outdated furniture, disgusting floors. But everyone was staring at me. Eye to eye. A look of strong distaste. These people were judging me, I was sure. My heart beat faster and the air seemed thin.

How did I get here? I asked myself.

A cart flew past with lights flashing and horn beeping. From another direction, a flight crew brushed by me, their make-up flawless and their hair tight. They rushed off to somewhere important, to serve drinks and make small talk with affluent businessmen. I whirled around and lost my sense of direction. I needed to get to where I was going, if only I knew where that was. It was at that moment I realized I had been walking in circles around the food court.

These people are definitely looking at me.

I scanned for a sign to the restroom. I might seem more normal if I was doing something with a purpose. Normal people go to the bathroom.

I sprinted across the walkway and rounded the corner to

the restroom. A young woman fixing her mascara glanced at me out of the corner of her eye. She was shaming me for my unkempt appearance—my two-month-old haircut and my faded jeans that had been worn ragged around the bottoms. I looked down to see my ugly brown shoes gazing up at me with their jagged leather and broken-down soles. They pleaded to be retired yet I found their loyalty and familiarity something I could not part with. I looked up at the girl, who continued to fix her makeup.

I definitely don't belong here.

I exited the restroom as quickly as I entered.

I was supposed to be headed somewhere, but I found myself walking aimlessly. I had time to spare before my flight, so after I made my way through the security checkpoint, I tried sitting on a bench and doing some work. However, my body was amped up, and I was incapable of sitting still. I needed to be physically doing something; I just didn't know what that something was. Pacing around the terminal, I walked faster as panic spidered its way through my veins.

Should I take an Ativan? I kept it on me for sleep, but it was also prescribed for anxiety. I was reluctant to take it though; I did not like feeling sedated. I spun around and then stopped.

No. There's a bar up there. I glanced toward the upper level of the food court.

The restaurant was decorated like a Mexican cantina, but pop music blared over the loudspeaker. The sign at the front bragged that they carried more than one hundred different kinds of tequila. A regional airport in the Midwest seemed like a strange place to find a world-class tequila bar.

Do I dare order liquor? I thought. *No, too strong.* I ordered a pint of beer instead. The bartender noticed my Michigan sweater and made some joke about the football game that took place the previous week. I nodded, put my headphones in my ears, and avoided the social interaction. My headphones had become my new best friend and the ultimate conversation killer. Earlier in the day, I had used them to stop some rather annoying small talk in the checked-baggage line.

I downed my beer and then signaled to the bartender to bring another.

I glanced at my phone. My flight was scheduled to depart in twenty minutes.

I need to go to my gate.

I chugged the second beer and left cash in the tumbler in front of me, cash because I didn't want Susan to know I was one of those people who drank at the airport. She was always telling me I drank too much.

The airport was more tolerable under my beer buzz. Nonetheless, the paranoia drew my attention, unnaturally, to every person I passed. I fixated on their eyes.

Why is everyone staring at me? I met every set of eyes, scanned the room. My gaze shifted back and forth. *Stop.* I focused on the floor—the gray tile floor—lining the walkway.

I wonder how many times they have mopped vomit up from this floor. I pictured the poor janitorial staff who had to clean up after all of these passengers, many of whom must have been sick or hungover or pregnant. Humans were a disgusting species.

I arrived at the gate to find passengers crowding the jetway.

The attendant had already called my zone, so I snuck into the middle of the line. I boarded the plane, placed my backpack in the overhead compartment, and took my seat in the first row. The plane was a regional jet, which meant there was no first class. To my disappointment, "1C" was just an ordinary seat behind the cockpit. There would be no special drink service or premium snacks this time.

An Indian man sat in the seat next to me. He wore a mint-green button-up shirt, forest-green pants, and black dress shoes. His hair had turned mostly gray. Having made several Indian friends during grad school and during my time as a faculty member, I generally held a favorable opinion of people from India. In this particular instance though, my anxiety put me in a panic, and I immediately associated this man with being, of all things, a terrorist.

He is going to kill me. He is going to take out a massive knife he snuck through security, and he is going to stab me. No, he is going to decapitate me. Saw my head off and hold it up for the whole plane to see. Then he will burst into the cockpit and fly the plane into the ground.

As the scene played out in my mind, my body began to shake, and my left hand gripped the armrest. I could see the warm blood dripping from my severed head and forming a pool next to my lifeless body, which lay on the scratchy blue carpet of the airplane. The passengers let out gasps and screams in terror, but none of them had the courage to confront the man, who had assumed the position of taking their lives.

Stop, I told myself forcefully. *The chances of something like that happening to me are slim. You are catastrophizing.*

I pulled out my headphones and plugged them into my phone, turning on music in an attempt to calm myself. The plane had finished boarding and the flight attendant pulled the cabin door closed. Through my music, I heard the overhead speaker providing the standard safety information, but I also heard someone mumbling. I pulled the headphones from my ears. The man was humming to himself.

He's praying! A last prayer before he musters up the courage to take down the plane. He has it all planned out. He is going to slaughter me and then kill all of these innocent people.

My heart pounded wildly as the plane started to taxi. I looked at the compartment above me and considered whether I should get up and take my Ativan even though the seatbelt sign was clearly on.

No. You are fine. Nothing is going to happen.

The man continued humming. I placed the headphones back in my ears and lay my head back against the seat. I gripped the armrest even more tightly, and I closed my eyes hard. The vision of my being decapitated played over again in gruesome detail. The sawing, the blood, my severed head being held up high in the air. Because I was in the first row, I could see the door to the cockpit.

He will have no trouble unlocking that metal mess. He just needs the code, which I'm sure any flight attendant will give him. Should I tell them? I feel like I should tell someone. The flight crew could totally prevent this if they only knew about it. After all, he only has a knife.

Despite believing it was prudent to tell someone, I held back. I had no proof that this man was a terrorist or even had a knife. I was certain I would not be taken seriously if I reported that the man sitting next to me was planning to cut my head off and then crash the plane. That sliver of logic held me in my seat. Instead, I tried to fight the anxiety by giving in.

If we're going down, we're going down. There is nothing I can do to stop something like this.

I turned the volume up on my music and attempted to relax. I gave in to the reality I was absolutely powerless to stop a murder, whether it was a school shooting or a terrorist attack. It was Rachel's logic, really; while we had discussed at length all the horrific situations my mind could imagine, Rachel absolutely refused to tell me everything would be fine. In fact, we always landed on the truth that horrible things can and do happen in this world, and there was nothing she could say that would protect me. I could not overreact in every situation I felt threatened, whether the threat was justified or not. More importantly, I could not act irrationally and blame some man who probably was not a real danger to me or anyone else. I listened to my music and turned my mind off, accepting the fact that I had no control over when and how I would die.

Fortunately, it was a short flight to Detroit. I held my breath during the landing and inhaled deeply as the plane's wheels touched the ground. The plane taxied to the gate, and I was the first person on the plane to unbuckle my seatbelt. I reached up and grabbed my backpack from the overhead bin. While I stood at the cabin door waiting for the jet bridge to attach, I looked over to see that the man continued to hum softly and smile out the window from his seat. For a moment, I had a change of heart.

I'll bet he is thinking about his family.
Then the door opened and my twisted reality returned.

Therapy (Part 5)

November 2014

I set my laptop on the couch and folded it open. I drew in deeply and then pushed the button to turn the computer on.

"There's no going back now," I said aloud even though no one else was home. Susan had taken Skye to her mother's house in Indiana for the weekend. Our nephew was celebrating his sixth birthday, and Susan made a case for Skye to go so she could spend time with her family. I fully agreed, but I used my work as an excuse to stay home. I had another motive though. Rachel, who saw how my fear of school shootings was destroying my ability to work, suggested doing intensive therapy to help me overcome my prior experiences at Virginia Tech. The timing was actually quite good because having Susan and Skye away would give me the time and space to heal. In an unusual move, Rachel scheduled me for three sessions within a week. She cautiously explained the process would be intense and difficult, but in the end would leave me feeling better. I was a little skeptical, but I complied because I was desperate. Seeing beheadings and the gunning down of students was becoming a regular occurrence, and I could not tolerate it any longer.

After our first session, Rachel tasked me with a most difficult activity: to research the Virginia Tech incidents in as much detail as possible. There were three separate incidents I needed to study—the escaped prisoner, the shooting, and the decapitation—and each event was increasingly difficult for me to face. Nonetheless, I logged into the computer and opened the browser. Then, I typed "William Morva" into the search engine. Images of the scruffy man in shackles appeared, followed by the familiar headlines from 2006. I opened my journal to the first blank page and began taking notes. There was not much to the Morva incident to note aside from my experience of driving down the highway on my way to campus, where I saw police officers standing with rifles every fifty yards. It was not long before I found an image matching my recollection. After receiving confirmation my experience was real and not imagined, I was ready to move on to the shooting.

Next, I typed "Virginia Tech" in the browser and allowed autocomplete to add the word "shooting." I first visited Wikipedia, which gave a very detailed timeline of the events that unfolded the morning of April 16. Then I searched news articles, and I was surprised to find details I had forgotten, like the name of the dormitory where the first shooting occurred and the names of the individuals who had lost their lives. Seeing the time gap between the dormitory shooting and the shootings at Norris Hall reminded me of the controversial alerts the university sent out, which downplayed the first shooting as an isolated incident and did not ask students to stay away from other parts of campus that day.

"I have those emails," I said aloud. "Where's that hard drive?"

I reached for my backpack and grabbed the trusty external hard drive that had saved my dissertation mere weeks before my Ph.D. defense. I had backed up my Virginia Tech email on that same hard drive. For some unknown reason, I had saved any and every email related to the shooting.

As I opened my email and scanned the messages from the date of the shooting, my search became dreadfully personal. Because I had the series of communications at my fingertips, I was able to essentially relive my experiences from 2007. Tears escaped the corners of my eyes as I read the university alerts, paying special attention to the timestamp appearing on each. The information the university sent out was too little and too late.

As I read further, I discovered the emails about the memorial services on the days after the shooting. An image flashed of my sullen form standing in a low-ceilinged room packed with members of my department. I recalled the head of the department breaking down in tears as he attempted to offer words of condolence to our shattered community. I remember thinking how awful it must have been to lead a department that had lost so many students and even a faculty member. And as I recalled these details, I cried even harder.

I ran to the bathroom for a tissue.

Names. What were their names?

I was surprised at how my memory had faded. I turned back to the browser and searched for information about the people who had lost their lives. The professor who held the door closed while students jumped from the classroom window. The high-performing undergraduate student who took the chance of registering for a difficult graduate class only to lose his life during the lecture. Their faces had been etched in my mind—people I had never even met yet they were so familiar to me.

I came across a photo of the temporary memorial that was put together just after the shooting. An anonymous person or group of people laid "Hokie stones"—i.e., blocks of granite—in a semi-circle on the Drill Field for each of the thirty-two victims. The memorial sat directly in front of Burress Hall; Burress Hall was adjacent to the site of the shooting.

Norris Hall.

In my mind, I could see the outside of the stone building from all angles. I had walked past the building hundreds of times on my way to and from Patton Hall, where the Civil and Environmental Engineering Department was housed. Norris Hall had haunted my dreams for nearly a decade. Its icy walls sent chills through my veins.

I need to see it. I need to find a photograph of the inside, of the classrooms.

I paused for a moment before proceeding. Rachel said I needed to study the shooting in as much detail as possible, but I wondered if perhaps I was going to make things worse by actually going to the site of the shooting in my search for images of the classrooms. I was already in too deep though.

You are already drowning. Do it.

I turned to my laptop and continued my search until I

found what I needed—photos of the insides of one of the classrooms. The photos were actually part of an article that had been published in the *Roanoke Times* on the renovations of the Norris Hall classrooms on the day of their reopening to the public. I stared at an image of a sterile classroom, walls painted white. The front of the room held a whiteboard. There was no furniture. The gothic windows lined the far end of the room, but, to my surprise, sunlight splayed across the floor in an unnaturally promising way. It was as if the shooting could never have taken place in that classroom. There was talk of repurposing the classrooms for communal space, but I had serious doubts that anyone would ever willingly linger in that place.

As the emotions reached a peak, I took a moment to release. I let out a loud, blubbering cry that blurred my eyes and caused my nasal passages to swell. It was as if the emotional scars that formed over time had been ripped open once again. I lay on the hardwood floor of my living room, shaking in grief, pausing only momentarily to grab another tissue. I was completely dismantled, and all I could think was, *Thank god Susan and Skye aren't here to see this.*

After several minutes, I regrouped. I jotted some notes in my journal, which I intended to share with Rachel when I saw her again in a couple of days. *Only one more tragedy to unearth*, I thought as the nausea overtook me. I typed "Virginia Tech decapitation" in the browser and immediately began hyperventilating.

The problem with the decapitation was that it was so sickeningly brutal I only half-believed it happened in the first place. My denial allowed me to chalk up the violent images to my sick imagination. However, once I began searching the web, the news articles would confirm my biggest fear, which was the murder actually happened and it happened *exactly* as I recalled.

Breathe. There is nothing to read that you don't already know. Get what you need, and then get out of here.

I quickly scanned through news articles until I could confirm what I needed to know about the murder. Once finished, I cleared my browsing history and shut down my computer.

My breath came in heaving sobs that crushed me. I lay on the couch and cried, wondering how I had been caught in the middle of such a violent storm. I wasn't even on campus when these things happened and look at the damage that was done. If I was this bad, what about the tens of thousands of others who were a part of that same community? And how deep must the trauma be for the students and teachers who were *actually* there? All because of the actions of three individuals. I shook my head over and over as though I could shake the sickness from my body.

It was a moment when I might normally self-medicate with alcohol, but Rachel had distinctly instructed me to take care of myself, which meant I needed to make sure I ate, rested, and avoided alcohol. Given we were in the midst of a rather intensive treatment, I decided to follow her instructions. After an hour of crying, I was fully exhausted, but nightmares instantly flooded my mind, scenes that were eerily familiar to the nightmares I used to have when I lived in Virginia.

I resigned myself to a night of tossing and turning in sheer terror.

Rachel led me down to her office, and we both took a seat. I hadn't slept in three days because I was awakened by disturbing nightmares every time I closed my eyes. "Perfecting the nightmare" is what I called Rachel's little therapy technique because it dredged up all of the fears and emotions of the events while filling in any gaps left by my fading memory. I was not sure what to expect in this second session with Rachel because it seemed like I had completely wrecked myself and had no hope of coming back.

"I need to be honest with you," Rachel began. "I know I said I would do the intensive trauma therapy with you today but—"

She paused, trying to find the right words.

"—I don't think I'm ready."

Surely she isn't backing out, I thought. Then I realized we had already started the process. In fact, I had spent the past several nights waking in terror. I could not allow it to end like this.

"I can refer you to someone who is really quite good who can help you with your PTSD—"

"Wait," I said. "What do you mean?"

"I'm so sorry. I thought I could do this, but I don't think I can."

My heart sunk. Rachel hadn't flinched once in our months of working together when I mentioned the twisted, violent thoughts that passed through my head. She never let on that the subject of my trauma made her uncomfortable. And now I was in the midst of hell—my wounds ripped freshly open and bleeding—and Rachel was backing out. I was totally dismayed but, I acted like I wasn't bothered.

"That's okay," I said quietly and looked at the floor. Rachel had already heard the worst of it—what I had brought with me to her office was merely the evidence to back up my experiences. After my web search the prior evening, I had been dried of all emotion and I was only left with an ability to relay facts. I took a deep breath as I prepared to break the news that Rachel and I needed to finish what we had started. "But we kind of need to do something about this big can of worms that I opened this week."

I opened my journal and pulled out a few sheets of paper, which were folded between the pages.

"What's this?" Rachel asked as I handed them to her.

"Those are the emails," I explained. "The first few are the alerts the university sent when the shooting happened, and the next ones are emails sent afterwards, about memorials and so on. The last one is an email I sent to the grad students in my department. You know, I was the departmental representative to the Graduate Student Assembly, and since my department was so deeply affected by the shooting, I wanted to share information to our students about how things like graduation would be affected. I remember at the time wanting to feel like I was doing something helpful. We were all so powerless..."

Rachel took a few minutes to read the emails, occasionally muttering or shaking her head. In the midst of reading the alerts, she said, "I can see so many things that they did wrong in these emails, from a mental health perspective."

"Yeah, mental health wasn't exactly Virginia Tech's strong suit," I joked, thinking about my own experiences with the counseling center on campus.

Rachel continued reading, and as she finished the last of the emails, she said, "Wow." Her response echoed in the stillness between us in her small lower-level office. I felt a sense of pride that I could share such a unique piece of history with Rachel, but at the same time, the hard copy of the email exchange made the connection between the shooting and me undeniably real.

"I haven't slept since I dug all of this up. I can't stop the nightmares..." I said, and the tears burned. A small sob escaped.

Rachel reached for the box on the end table and offered a tissue to me. I grabbed one and blew my nose. Then she said, "Okay, we'll do this."

We spent the hour going over the details I had uncovered in my search and discussing the emotions they brought out in me. It was painful. Rachel, despite showing an initial hesitation, maintained her stalwart appearance and was spot on in her technique.

At the end of the session, Rachel stressed the importance of self-care over the next several days. "It will be difficult for a few days, but eventually you will start to see the nightmares and anxiety diminish," she said. "I will see you again on Wednesday. It's really just to check in and make sure that you are doing okay, but I honestly think you are going to be fine."

"Thanks," I said, and I stood up from the couch.

"Good job today," she said and patted my shoulder as I walked past.

"You too." I smiled weakly.

Discovering a Way to Stop Time

December 2014

A month passed following the intensive therapy with Rachel. I suffered through several more days of nightmares, but eventually they faded enough that I could sleep. As I entered my classroom each week, a new strength filled me, a new certainty that a brutal murder was *not* going to take place. It was a feeling I had not felt in a long time. Nevertheless, my bipolar disorder was still uncontrolled, and it was not long before I could feel myself slipping into psychosis again. It was the creature lurking in the shadows near the trash bin. The distant voices outside the living room window. The dim figures in the corners of my eyes. It was no longer trivial that my productivity slipped over the past several days. I began to stare blankly at the wall in my office, unable to move for minutes—maybe even hours—at a time. I became suspicious of others—not a specific threat that could be quantified, but a general uneasiness as if there was a certain conspiring malevolence behind the eyes of strangers. I was aware my world was shifting, but I was unable to counteract the momentum distorting my reality. Each day, I found myself more and more inside my head. The bizarre was becoming increasingly plausible, and the laws of physics had become malleable, allowing for an alternate reality that suited my supernatural thinking.

I drove to work in the early morning, my hair still damp from the shower and the corner of my mouth flavored with mint toothpaste. Outside was dim and blue, a cloudy December sky just before dawn. Snowflakes drifted; winter was upon us. From the driver's seat of the minivan, my eyes darted from passing car to passing car, taking snapshots of the ongoing traffic. My mind moved swiftly to find meaning behind the pattern of vehicles on the road.

Yes, it does seem possible... if I focus enough... if I can just project my frame of reference onto another moving object, like, say, that car right there... yes... I will be able to stop time.

Ingenious. It was the kind of discovery that would transform the field of physics. It was worthy of a medal. No, it was worthy of a Nobel Prize! I focused with great intensity on the oncoming traffic, glancing back and forth between the clock on the dashboard and the cars that were whizzing by. The faster they traveled, the slower time moved.

Aha! Time travel is most certainly possible. All I need to do is prove it, to prove that I have stopped time by projecting my frame of reference onto another moving object. I just need an equation. A mathematical proof. I've read of something similar to this. What was it called? Ah, yes. Einstein's Theory of Relativity.

A faint glimmer of sanity appeared. A brief realization that perhaps it was delusional thinking driving me to such uncharted territory. A "wait, you are a structural engineer, not a physicist" kind of thought. For a moment, I paused and questioned whether I should allow myself to follow this line of thinking, which I could recognize as being unusual, even for me.

However, an overwhelming desire to explore this fascinating new territory immediately squashed the reality check. The racing thoughts again took over.

I am a genius! It is my job as an academic to come up with radically new theories. This is the kind of discovery that brings fame. Run with it, Ann! You are onto something!

I drove rapidly to campus and parked the van. The sky had brightened, coloring the world in a less-dramatic shade of blue. I hurried to my office, an occasional snowflake kissing my eyelashes. I pulled my hand out of my coat pocket and wiped my wet face.

In the building, I turned the corner and rushed down the hallway, hoping none of my colleagues would interrupt me. Inside my office, I pulled out my laptop without even bothering to remove my winter coat. I opened the browser and typed "Theory of Relativity" into the search engine. I scanned quickly through the text, digging for the concepts supporting my new theory. My leg tapped rapidly as I read. I had found my proof.

"Time dilation. Time appears slower to an object moving at a higher velocity."

I began scribbling notes in my journal.

"December 5, 2014. I think I have discovered a way to stop time. All you need to do is to project your frame of reference onto another moving object. If you do it enough—many times back to back, such as with vehicles on your way home from work—time almost stands still."

Then, like a true scientist, I sought to come up with an experiment that would allow me to test my new hypothesis. However, I was quickly discouraged by my lack of a solution. I jotted a few more ideas in my journal.

I want to devise an experiment, but I think it may be impossible to test because time cannot be separated from the individual experiencing it. It's like when time stops in a waiting room, but only for the individual who is waiting. The rest of the world keeps moving.

Several hours passed as my wheels continued to spin on the concept of time dilation. My inability to articulate a rational hypothesis was disheartening, and by the end of the day, I walked away from any serious attempt at pursuing research on the subject. I wrote a final thought in my journal.

"Time dilation: time appears slower to an object (my mind) moving at a faster velocity (racing thoughts)."

In other words, the only thing I was able to prove was that time appeared to move slowly to a sick individual—*me*—who was experiencing racing thoughts caused by bipolar mania. I had wasted an entire day coming to this conclusion, and my colleagues would surely laugh if they knew I was working on something like this. My heart descended like a coin in a fountain.

The End

December 2014

I lay on the couch, unable to lift my head. To even blink was too demanding of a task. Susan and Skye moved quickly about me as though they were stuck in a film whose frames were accelerated by a factor of four. Susan made dinner. Skye and Susan ate. Susan did the dishes. Skye played quietly on the floor. Susan took a load of laundry downstairs. Susan got Skye a snack. And all the while, I lay motionless on the couch.

Susan sat down on the loveseat and, looking up from her phone, she finally said, "There's a sale going on at Weber's Inn. If you book a room between December twenty-sixth and thirtieth, you can get a poolside room for only one hundred and ten bucks." I didn't lift my head, so she followed up with, "Staycation?" Her suggestion was a good one. Skye was out of preschool for the holidays, and we had decided not to travel to visit family. For some reason, we believed that Christmas at home would be good for once. However, we were only a few days in and already overcome by a serious case of cabin fever. I appreciated Susan was trying to make it a nice break, but my heart was not in it.

"Okay," I said blankly.

Sensing my lack of enthusiasm, Susan followed up with, "Come on. It'll be fun. Skye would love to go swimming, and she gets so excited when we stay in a hotel."

"Yeah, that's fine." It was all I could muster.

"So I'll book a room for tomorrow?"

"Okay."

I wasn't well. After my Einstein moment, I had succumbed to the blackness of my mind. My medications weren't helping, and it seemed there weren't many options left. My illness was destroying my life at home and work. I was, more than ever, a burden on Susan. I could not be relied on for anything. When she asked me to do dishes, I failed her. When she asked me to pick up something at the store, I failed her. When she expected me to put Skye to bed, I failed her. The only thing I could reliably do was lay on the couch and stare out the window, and Susan didn't hesitate to let me know I was letting her down. Even though the holidays were supposed to be a time of joy, I had never felt a greater despair. I did nothing but cause my loved ones pain. The world would have been a better place without me in it.

The following day, as we prepared for our staycation, Susan began to get frustrated that I was not doing my part. She was busy packing the suitcase, while I lay on the couch.

"Do you not want to go?" she said.

"No, I want to go, I just don't feel well." I huffed loudly.

"What do you mean you don't 'feel well'?"

"I don't know. I mean, I just don't want to do *anything*." Then, realizing that she might take it in the wrong way, I added, "I want to go, I want to spend time with you and Skye, but I just don't have the energy."

She let out an exasperated sigh. "You don't do *anything* anymore. I can't even get you to pay the daycare bill, let alone do the dishes or a load of laundry. I'm *tired*," she yelled as her foot stomped against the floor. "I'm tired of doing *everything* around here. I thought a staycation would be something nice that we could do as a family." Then, she pleaded, "Can't you do this for Skye?"

"Ugh," I moaned. "*Yes*, I can do this for Skye." My voice had escalated to a level that matched hers. "But it's *hard*. Don't you get it? I'm depressed. *I can't help it.*"

"Whatever," Susan said. And then, in her all-or-nothing attitude, she said through clenched teeth, "We're not going."

She had turned the situation into it being *my fault* Skye was not going to get to stay at the hotel with the big swimming pool. Skye would be devastated. I grew furious.

"No, you and Skye go. I will stay here. You promised she would get to go. You and I clearly can't get along. You go. Take her. Leave me." All at once, I felt the rush of energy like that day I climbed a twenty-foot ladder to the roof of the barn to fetch a toy for Skye. The ladder vibrated with each shaking step and, as I neared the top, I realized how fragile life was, how a gust of wind could blow the ladder sideways and slam my body on the gravel driveway below. That was how bones broke. That was how people died. There was a moment separating life from death.

The uneasy feeling was accompanied by a dialogue that was going on in the back of my mind.

Look at you. You are ruining your family. You are a waste.

You are nothing but trouble. The world would be a better place without you in it. Send them away.

This was it. I needed to get them out of the house. This was it. This was the time to end it all, to rid my family of my burden. I did nothing but make everyone miserable. I was plagued by this horrid illness, which was clearly incurable. Perhaps I was not even sick; perhaps I was just seeking attention. Then again, I had seen the demon. I heard the music. The voices. The bees. I was a monster. These things made me terrified to be alive.

I'm sick. But I can't be treated. Death is the only hope.

I stormed off, threw myself onto the bed. Energy thrummed through me. I wanted to start smashing mirrors and throwing picture frames and tearing drawers from dressers, but I held back.

Send them away.

My blood was boiling, my heart pounding with excitement.

Send them away, and then get the bottles of pills from the medicine cabinet. Start with the Ativan. It is strong. It will make you sleep. It will be easy. One pill. Two pills. A handful of pills. Wash them down with water. You can call 9-1-1. Leave it to the fates as to whether you live or die. Hopefully, it is the latter.

As I flustered with excitement that I would finally have the chance to kill myself, Susan rushed into the bedroom. She scooped up the suitcase, its contents hanging out of the unzipped sides. In a sour tone, she said, "I'm not going to let you ruin this for Skye. We are going. You can stay here if you want."

This is it! A few more minutes and then they will be gone.

I tried to wrap my mind around what was happening. Rachel and I had discussed suicide ad nauseam over the past year. Her advice was, "Tell someone if you are having thoughts of suicide, and if you ever have a *plan*, you need to go directly to the hospital." While I did have a plan, I could only tell if I was *seriously* considering suicide if I started downing pills. I thought of my plan as a compromise: call 9-1-1 when you *act*. But I knew it was not enough.

I heard the muffled talking of Susan and Skye in the other room. Susan was explaining something to Skye, and Skye clearly was not happy about it. She burst through the bedroom door.

"Mama! Mommy says you aren't going with us," she pouted.

"No, Skye," I said in my best attempt at a normal tone. *Get out. Get out so I can do it.* "Mama doesn't feel well."

"Oh," she whined. "But you said you would come!" She crossed her arms firmly and stomped her feet.

I let out a puff of air. All I wanted was to be left alone, but my resolve to be a good parent had taken over. I couldn't do it, not today, not with Skye standing by and counting on me. A tear rolled down my cheek, and, in an instant, I began sobbing.

"I'll come, Skye." I sniffled and then said quietly to her, "Let me talk to Mommy."

I got up from the bed and called out, "Wait! Susan, don't go. Don't leave me." *This can't be it,* my mind shifted. *I can't leave them.*

I sniffled, calling to Susan desperately. "Don't leave me *alone*." I had a wildness in my eyes that was uncharacteristic of me. She looked at me as though she no longer recognized the creature that stood before her. I gently grabbed her arm with both of my hands and pulled her shoulder to my face. She resisted at first, but then softly wrapped her other arm around me. I collapsed into the safety and warmth of her embrace.

"I'm so sorry," I repeated over and over again, as I cried uncontrollably.

"I know," she said, as a tear rolled down to her chin.

After several minutes, I caught my breath. *You have to tell her. To keep you safe.*

"Tonight was going to be the night," I whispered. "I was planning to take pills, to overdose. I wanted you and Skye to leave so I could do it." I sniffled. My hands were shaking. "It's bad."

I gripped her shirt tightly and pressed my soggy face into her shoulder as though she was the only thing holding me to earth.

"I don't know what to *do* anymore." I wept furiously, gripping Susan tightly.

"Oh, Ann," she said as another tear trickled from her eye. She reached her arm around me in an attempt to console me.

"I can't be alone right now. I don't trust myself." Then, I added, "And I don't want Skye to not get to stay at the hotel." Skye, my reason for being. She had, on more than one occasion, brought me away from the ledge that separated life from death. She needed me to be well. Wiping my face, I said, "I promise I won't fight any more. I'm sorry this even happened."

"I'm sorry too," she said, "for being hard on you. Look, let's get packed up."

"Okay," I said and sniffled one last time.

After arriving at the hotel, we went directly to the pool. Susan and Skye swam, while I sat in a chair on the edge of the water. I forced a smile as Skye shouted, "Hey, Mama! Watch this!" and jumped from the side of the pool into Susan's arms.

"Good job!" I shouted back.

My smile faded and my stare wandered from my family to the choppy surface of the pool. I was entranced by the sharp peaks that rose and fell with the movements of Susan and Skye in the water. As I saw myself submerged beneath the water, fighting for oxygen, the waves whispered, *You almost did it. You almost did it this time.*

A chill ran up my spine, and I shuddered.

After we returned to the room, Susan got Skye into her pajamas. Skye quickly fell into a deep slumber in her bed. I opened the bottle of wine we brought with us and poured it into two disposable plastic cups. Susan proceeded with a thoughtful and supportive tone, but she nonetheless was cautious. It was the first time I had planned to act on suicide, and it no doubt scared her. As we drank, Susan and I lay next to each other. We talked about what had happened earlier in the evening, and we talked about what had been happening to me over the past several months. I told her how I had never been more scared. I told her how I no longer trusted myself, that on more than one occasion I had thought about hurting myself and, a few times, almost did hurt myself. I told her about many of the troubling hallucinations and paranoia that I had experienced and kept secret from her. Unlike most of our interactions, Susan listened quietly, her words affirming rather than questioning. It was the first time that I felt able to tell her about the gravity of the illness, how it had destroyed me at home and at work and how I was beginning to believe that there was no way out. As we had finished the bottle of wine, I curled up in Susan's arms and softly cried myself to sleep.

The Fallout

December 2014

I sat on the couch and filled my pillbox, patiently counting out the pills for each of the four medications I was now taking for the bipolar disorder: Lamictal, Prozac, Invega, and now, a touch of Lithium. Dr. Park stated that Lithium was known to reduce the risk of suicide in patients with bipolar disorder, and, because it was a mood stabilizer, she said that it would also help to combat the depression. I dumped a single pill of Lithium in my hand. Would this small capsule be enough to save my life, to pull me out of a place where I was destined to burst into flames? The future seemed so dim, so distant from me. I squeezed my hand tightly around the pill and closed my eyes, making a wish like a child might make upon the candles of her birthday cake.

Keep me alive.

Then, I dropped the pink capsule into Sunday's slot, and I finished filling the rest of the pillbox.

I put all of the pill bottles in a Ziploc baggy and carried them to the bedroom.

"Susan?"

"Yes," she said in a muffled voice. She was in the bathroom

brushing her teeth, the foam of the toothpaste oozing out the sides of her mouth.

"I need you to take these. Hide them somewhere I will not find them." I held out the Ziploc baggy. "I don't trust myself around them."

Susan rinsed her mouth and dried it on the hand towel that hung on the wall.

"Okay." Her eyes were fixed on mine as she attempted to gauge my well-being. I was no longer a threat to myself, but it would take some time before I could convince Susan of that.

"Thanks." I turned away and then paused. "It was Rachel's suggestion. To keep me safe."

"Good call," she said.

"Yeah." I walked to the kitchen, grabbed the pillbox from the counter, and dumped Sunday's contents into my hand. It sure seemed like a large quantity of pills, but as I looked at my hand, I could see a purpose for each pill.

This one is my mood stabilizer. And this one is for the depression. This one is my antipsychotic. And this one—well—it may just save my life.

I tossed the handful of pills in my mouth and downed them with a glass of water, tolerating the few that stuck to the insides of my mouth. I took another gulp and swallowed the bitter taste of my medications.

The next day, a fog seeped over me like a heavy blanket. I slept a lot throughout the day. When I was able, I tried to interact with Skye, but the new dose of Lithium made me tired. I spent a lot of time on the couch and occasionally went back to the bedroom to rest undisturbed. Instead of sleeping,

I spent most of the time mulling over what had happened. My eyes, which were puffy from crying, stung as though I had grains of sand in them. I could not quite grasp the notion I had legitimately planned to overdose. I shuddered at the idea that, had I attempted it, I would have ended up in the hospital or, quite possibly, dead. In my imagination, I approached death as though a giant eraser was going to come down from the sky and quietly remove me from my family. I wanted to be taken from my life in a way that would allow Susan and Skye to go about their lives as if I had never existed. The reality was that suicide did not happen quietly. It shattered the fundamental structures of life. *Someone* would have found my body on the bathroom floor. It would have been Susan. And she would have had Skye with her. And who knew what kind of mess an overdose left behind?

More troubling to me was the fact that, although I was no longer seriously considering a suicide attempt, I still was not well. I was not actively thinking about taking my life, but at the same time, I could not see a future for myself. I lacked a desire to do anything. It was all I could do to lift myself from the couch and take a drink of water or, occasionally, eat. Instead of embracing life, I buried my head in my pillow, closed my eyes, and waited for the illness to pass. Days passed without movement, and all I could think was, *Thank god it is winter break.*

Through it all, Susan gave me my space. She took care of the housework, cooked the meals, and tended to Skye. I didn't know if she understood that I needed the space to heal or if she was merely keeping the house running. Regardless, she gave me exactly what I needed. It was almost as if I was recovering from surgery in the way Susan took care of me. For that, I was most grateful.

Each day of my recovery became easier. My dark mood gradually lightened as the Lithium took hold. After a week or so, I found it easier to talk and to *smile*, and I found one day that my persistent thoughts of death eventually ceased. Being part of my family's activities was less and less of an effort, which was *amazing*; I was no longer glued to the couch each day. I had energy but not in a dangerous manic way. And I felt *normal* in a way I hadn't felt in a long time. The Lithium fog—which clouded my mind, making it hard to work or concentrate—lifted eventually, and my thinking became clearer too.

As we approached the New Year, we were greeted with some unseasonably warm weather. "Who wants to go to the park?" Susan asked one afternoon.

"Me!" shouted Skye.

"Good idea," I said.

"You don't have to come if you don't want to—"

"No, I'll come." I sat up quickly from the couch.

Skye ran up to give me a hug. "Yay, Mama!"

I laughed lightly and said, "Well, go get your shoes on, silly!" This light mood came easily to me these days, like an old friend who had merely lost her way.

We loaded up in the van and drove to a park near town that had a large, wooden play structure. As we pulled into a parking spot, Skye squirmed and shouted. I unbuckled her from the car seat and set her on the ground. There was only one other vehicle in the parking lot, signifying the days of going to the park were dreadfully limited with the arrival of winter. Skye bolted toward the play structure. I let her run ahead, recognizing there were no dangers to be had on this empty playground. I waited for Susan, and then the two of us walked to the playground together, the sun warm, shining on our faces. It felt good to be outside in the fresh air.

"Mama, come and get me," Skye yelled from the top of the structure.

Susan looked to me, questioning if I was capable of playing.

I paused a second and then yelled back, "Okay, here I come!"

We played for more than an hour, with me chasing Skye down slides and across rickety bridges. Susan sat on a bench and watched the two of us with amusement. Eventually I caught up to Skye. I grabbed her in a bear hug and growled as I lifted her off the ground. Skye laughed, while I reveled. I let her wrestle loose and run to another area of the playground.

"Can't catch me!"

"Here I come!" I called back.

After a while, Susan let us know it was time to get going. We did not have anywhere to be, but dinner would be coming soon. "How about if we eat out tonight?" Susan asked.

"The French Fry Place!" Skye shouted.

I laughed and said, "Yeah, the French Fry Place," which was our code name for a local vegetarian restaurant that only had one thing on the menu Skye would eat: French fries.

As we reached the van, Susan climbed behind the driver's seat. I buckled Skye into her car seat and then climbed into the passenger side.

Susan turned to me and said, "That was fun."

I said, "Yeah, it was, actually. I'm feeling pretty good. I think the meds are working." I was shocked to even say it. It had been such a long and despairing process. To actually see progress was an incredible feeling, one that was well overdue.

"I'm glad to hear it," she said. "Maybe tonight we can watch a movie."

Even though I had been fighting extreme tiredness, I was willing to fight to stay awake to spend time with Susan on this particular night.

"Yeah," I said. "It's a plan."

In the winter of 2015, my tenure package moved to the College of Engineering's Executive Committee for review. My push to add publications and funding to my CV in the previous year ultimately didn't change things for better or worse. What mattered most was the culmination of work those first six years, a period during which I had had many successes despite my struggles with infertility and mental illness. So while I was incredibly ill in 2013 and 2014, I had already done well enough in my career to meet the bar. Following the college's evaluation in 2015, I was promoted to Associate Professor with tenure at the University of Michigan. It was the single most important achievement of my career.

While I battled mental illness leading up to tenure, I never once disclosed to my employer my diagnosis, nor did I seek any sort of accommodation even though I may have benefited from a leave of absence or a release from teaching. The stigma around mental illness was too great, and the advice I received from Rachel was to conceal my illness from my employer as much as I could. Hence, I taught my classes and supervised my students in research despite my illness. It was a real challenge, and the process was incredibly isolating. When I learned about my promotion in 2015, I vowed to use the job security of tenure to advocate for those with mental illness and other disabilities.

Teaching became much easier following my therapy sessions with Rachel. The intense trauma therapy greatly helped to correct the thought distortions left from the Virginia Tech traumas. Following 2014, I rarely had PTSD flashbacks while teaching, which undoubtedly made the job easier and, dare I say, more enjoyable. I needed to be mindful of my exposure to the news, which was triggering, as well as certain situations, like being in crowds, which still provoked anxiety. However, the anxiety was far more manageable than what I experienced prior to treatment. It was an anxiety that could be managed with deep breaths and mindfulness, one that didn't involve visions of bullets and blood and death.

I underwent tweaks in my medication for several months. I tried one or two more antipsychotic medications before my doctor found one that curbed the psychosis completely for me. It was a gradual process that required several adjustments to the dose, but eventually one day the voices stopped calling my name and I was no longer paranoid all the time. What's more, under the Lithium, I no longer experienced suicidal thoughts. Dr. Park eventually moved out of state, and my new psychiatrist ended up increasing the Lithium to the therapeutic level and coming off Lamictal completely. It is important to stress that medication regimes for people with bipolar disorder are as unique to the individual as their fingerprint, hence all the trial and error. While Lithium was the gold standard treatment for bipolar disorder, Lamictal—an anti-convulsant, of all things—was an up-and-coming mood stabilizer that had great successes in regulating mood and didn't require all the lab work. While it didn't work in my case, it was worth trying. It is also worth pointing out the effectiveness of medications can change over time, meaning that what worked for me in the past might not work for me at some point in the future. After much reading and discussion with my psychiatrists, I accepted these truths and committed to taking my medication daily as prescribed.

Therapy continued indefinitely. It took years before I became fully productive again. For a long time, my therapy sessions focused on helping me become a functioning adult at home and in the workplace. While the bipolar symptoms subsided, I had trouble focusing from the medications, and I was tired all the time. I kept Rachel as my therapist because she turned out to be a really good fit for what I needed, but I also reached out to people in online forums for advice. I befriended several people with serious mental illness, including a woman with schizophrenia, who helped me understand and reconcile my differences with the psychosis. I eventually stopped beating myself up every time I had a hallucination and instead accepted it as part of my reality. The truth was I had a psychotic disorder brought about by an illness of my brain, and there was no shame in that. From then on, I embraced the psychosis and used it as a tool to measure when I needed an adjustment in medication.

Following that night at the hotel in December 2014, I vowed to be more open and honest with Susan about my mental illness. I promised to share more about my experience but in a way that did not overwhelm her. I told her I'd let her know what I needed from her in terms of support, acknowledging we were a partnership that couldn't function if I was keeping things from her. In therapy, Rachel helped me prioritize things at home so as to keep Susan happy with me. I managed to do *some* housework tasks here and there, and to make up for my shortcomings, I'd pick up flowers or some other small token for Susan. Thus, I showed love to Susan even in times when I was incapable of doing so in more typical ways.

As Susan said months before, we would no longer try to get pregnant and instead would focus on adoption. We agreed to wait until I was better, even if it took years. There was no rush; Skye would have a sibling at some point in the future. For the time-being, I focused on my recovery. And that was just fine by me.

Epilogue

March 2017

At the end of the driveway, I brought the truck to a halt and jumped out. I began unloading the bags of trash and recycling from the bed of the truck into the bins. A warm wave of spring air blew past me, rustling the leaves under the bushes. The sky was cloudless—not in its usual foreboding way, but rather in a way that told me everything was going to be fine. I was optimistic as I listened to the tree frogs chirping in the woods. The smell of bonfires and freshly mowed grass crept into my senses. It was going to be a great summer.

I paused for a moment before slamming the gate of the truck closed and climbing into the driver's seat. Susan would be home any minute with the kids. I needed to finish getting the house ready. Our adoption worker was coming by at four o'clock for our final home visit. We had come full circle from attempting to get pregnant to my falling ill with bipolar disorder to my recovery, which made possible the adoption of our long-awaited second child.

After parking the truck in the barn, I pulled out my phone to check for texts, emails—*anything*—related to the adoption. Mya had just turned one, and I was beyond anxious to get the adoption finalized. The beautiful little girl had come into our care when she was less than one week old. We had seen her first smile, her first crawl, her first tooth, her first steps. She came to us as a temporary ward of the state, and when her biological parents walked away, Susan and I were the first and only family in line to adopt. It was a long road we had traveled with much uncertainty, our outlook ranging anywhere from trepidation to hope in more than a year. In the excitement of a near-final adoption, we had completed all our medical forms, financial statements, and background checks. The adoption worker needed to visit once more before she could complete the adoption report and submit it to the state. It was a long haul, but Mya was worth it, without a doubt. She renewed my life purpose once again and, even on my darkest of days, she possessed the quality of being able to make me smile and feel loved, just as Skye always had.

No texts or emails, but I did receive a notification from *The New York Times* about a developing story of an attack in London. My stomach turned at the thought of violence. Following the episode I suffered in 2014 where my post-traumatic stress disorder from the Virginia Tech shooting reared its ugly head, I had been unable for years to read the news. In 2016, I felt I was finally well enough to resume nearly all of my normal activities, but reading the news was still difficult. Over a span of a few years, the world had become an even less safe place, a place where violence had taken the form of trucks running through crowds of innocent people. As I pondered the London attack, my chest hurt with the notion people had been injured—people had *died*—in yet another horrific terrorist attack. Not to mention, the attack took place in a city I frequented.

You don't need to go there, Rachel whispered. *You have been there, and you have since moved on.*

I closed my eyes and took a breath. The incident was sad. It was tragic. But it was not my fight. Instead of opening the article, I turned off the screen and slipped the phone into my back pocket. Today was not a day for distractions; it was a day for celebration, for Mya's sake and for my family's sake. I was beginning to learn I had little control over what happened in the world, and no amount of my worrying would lessen the damage caused by that truck in London.

I entered the house, and Jasper—our lab-terrier mix—barked eagerly. I rushed back to the bedroom, grabbed his leash, and wrestled it onto his collar. I had no idea why we had gotten a dog at the same time Mya entered our life. I lacked the patience for a high-energy puppy, but the chaos he brought seemed fitting for the crazy life Susan and I had built. He was a black dog, and he made me wonder why depression had ever been referred to as "the black dog." His energy was, if anything, the exact opposite of depression.

Jasper dragged me to the back of the yard, right to the edge of the lawn where we allowed the grass to grow wild. The bat house hung proudly in the air, its black paint beginning to chip from the weather. In recent years, bats zigzagged across the dark summer skies snacking on mosquitos, reminding me that perhaps my crazy efforts were not a waste after all. In fact, so much good had come from my mania, and I owed many of my successes to those creative bursts that undoubtedly drew me towards academia. Having recently made my way through tenure at the University of Michigan, I was reminded of how ridiculously successful I was, and still at such a young age. The praise I received upon my promotion to Associate Professor was enough to override the self-doubt that plagued me most days. Nonetheless, I still struggled with bipolar disorder despite being what was referred to as "stable." My self-image was a reflection of my mood on any given day.

Jasper and I walked around the property line and then made a dash for the house. It was dinnertime for Jasper, and he knew it. As I took him to his crate in the bedroom and dumped a cup of kibble into his bowl, I heard the garage door open. A moment later, Skye burst into the house shouting, "Mama! Mama!"

I stepped into the living room. "What is it?"

"Look what I got today at the book fair!" she exclaimed as she pulled out a book about rocks. Skye wanted to be a "mad scientist" when she grew up. She excelled at math and had a passion for science. A small part of me wondered if she might grow up to be an engineer like me.

"Oh, cool!"

She grabbed a snack from the pantry and ran downstairs to watch cartoons. I frantically cleaned and straightened the living room, knowing that the worker would be there any moment.

Susan came in the door a minute later, lugging Mya in her car seat.

"Hey," I said to Susan.

"Hey, did you get all the paperwork in order?"

"Yeah, it's on the coffee table." She set Mya down in the living room and hurried off to freshen up.

"Hey there, baby girl," I said as I unbuckled the car seat.

Mya beamed back at me and let out a giggle.

"Let's get you something to eat." I carried her to the kitchen and set her in her highchair with a handful of graham crackers. She thanked me with a singsong "ba-ba-ba-ba."

As I turned away, I looked out the front window and saw a silver car coming up the driveway.

"She's here," I called out to Susan.

"Okay," Susan called back and hurried into the living area. I gathered our paperwork and then lifted Mya out of the highchair. My heart fluttered with nerves. The path of fostering-to-adopt Mya had been long and arduous. We had nearly reached the end, but, until the gavel fell, we knew nothing was certain. We felt Mya was "ours" from the day we met her in the hospital. Born to a drug addict who had a long history of having children removed from her care, Mya was the perfect foster care placement for us—she was an infant with a high likelihood of being available for adoption. She was the long-awaited child Susan and I had been trying for. She was the tiny being that made it all worth it—the fertility battles that had damaged my mental health so long ago, and the scars of trauma from our first two foster care placements that had transformed us from ordinary people into seasoned foster parents. Mya had overcome drug addiction in her first few days of life, and as she grew, she would face insurmountable learning difficulties due to her prenatal exposure to alcohol.

Susan let Julie, the adoption worker, in and brought her up

to the great room. Julie was a twenty-something-year-old with shoulder-length brown hair. Fresh out of college, she had a brightness about her that showed she had not yet been broken by the system, a system that failed damaged children and broke the hearts of anyone who legitimately cared for them, as Susan and I had learned.

Julie settled on the couch and pulled out a stack of papers from her briefcase, while Susan and I assembled our own stack of documents. Mya cruised along the edge of the coffee table, trying to grab anything and everything within reach. I got up and shadowed her around the room, grabbing things from her that were not suitable for a one-year-old—papers, wrappers, and Legos Skye had left lying around and that had been overlooked in our last-minute cleaning—and offering her age-appropriate snacks and toys. She was generally disinterested in baby things, but I followed her and did my best to keep her happy.

I handed Julie our paperwork. At the bottom of the stack was the mental health form my psychiatrist had completed. I was fearful my diagnosis of severe bipolar with psychosis would raise a red flag in our application for adoption. The mental health assessment form required by the state asked, among other things, "Would this individual be considered a stable and appropriate candidate to be an adoptive parent?" There was no doubt I excelled when it came to parenting, but whether I could be considered "stable" was perhaps debatable, even on medications and in therapy. However, my new psychiatrist, Dr. Hughes, and my long-time therapist, Dr. Rachel, were enthusiastically supportive of the adoption. As long as I was managing my symptoms with medications and therapy, the bipolar diagnosis was trivial in their eyes.

"Our financial documents are all in there," I said, as Julie flipped through the stack.

"Uh-huh." Social workers were so used to paperwork it was unnecessary for me to explain what I was handing to her. Still, I continued.

"And the form from my psychiatrist is at the bottom there." I swallowed.

"Great, it looks like I have everything I need," she said and gave a smile. "Do you have any questions for me, or is there anything you need?"

Susan looked at me and then back at Julie. "No, I think we're all good."

"Okay then, I'll get this submitted and will let you know when I hear back from Lansing so we can go ahead and get the adoption hearing scheduled with the court."

Susan and I stood up as Julie grabbed her things. We walked her to the door and said our goodbyes. As soon as the door was closed, Susan shrieked. "I can't believe this is it!"

"I know!" I said. I picked up Mya and spun her around, as she giggled. "Congratulations, little one!" I gave her a kiss on the cheek and then passed her over to Susan, who then gave Mya a big hug. I turned away and, with a look of bewilderment, said, "I can't believe this is happening. We are actually going to adopt Mya. She's going to be ours."

Susan corrected me, "She *is* ours."

"Yes, of course. She *is* ours."

I turned back to Susan, and I looked into Mya's two small

brown eyes. I saw the resilience and determination that had carried her so far in her short life. I could see her life ahead of her, and I saw a happiness I thought I could never imagine. Sure, there would be obstacles, but Mya was strong. And she had me in her life to care for her, comfort her, and watch her grow, something she wouldn't have had if I had allowed the mental illness to win. Despite all the pain and all the close calls, I was on my way to recovery. No doubt, my journey with mental illness would be lifelong—there would be missteps and relapses that would require lifestyle and medication adjustments—but I had found a way to *live* with bipolar disorder.

Acknowledgements

First and foremost, I would like to express my gratitude to my family for standing by me through this tumultuous time. Susan has been, and continues to be, my tether to reality. She stood by me through all of this and then supported my "crazy" idea to write and publish this book, even if it was a book she never wanted to read. She and I are still going strong, twenty-plus years since we first met. In addition, I am forever indebted to my three children, who have given my life meaning and hope. If it wasn't for "Skye," I may very well have given in to the illness. My kids are the center of my universe; they are my reason for living each and every day. I'd also like to thank my parents for always being there for me. Our relationship has evolved as a result of this experience, and I feel closer now that we communicate openly and honestly, especially in regards to mental health. My parents continue to be my biggest fans in all aspects of my career, my mom hanging my CV from her fridge until there were too many pages to hold up with a magnet and my dad cheering me on with each social media post.

I wouldn't be anywhere without the support of my colleagues at the University of Michigan. Rather than pushing me away following my disclosure of having bipolar disorder, my department, college, and university have supported my academic career while embracing my advocacy work related to mental health, and for that I am forever grateful. I would especially like to acknowledge Nancy Love, who was at Virginia Tech at the same time as me and helped me reconcile some of the trauma. Thanks to all of the administrators in the College of Engineering who stood by me through challenging times and helped me rebuild my research program following my recovery. I also would like to specifically thank the faculty and staff of the Department of Civil and Environmental Engineering at the University of Michigan, who have contributed to my academic success and made work an enjoyable place.

Dr. Rachel, my therapist of ten years now, deserves special recognition. When we first met in 2013, I was doubtful of the benefits of therapy. However, Rachel joined me on this incredible journey and brought me to the other end a stronger and more resilient person. I am grateful that Rachel never shied away from the darkest aspects of my mental illness and trauma, which helped normalize my deeply troubling experiences with psychosis and PTSD. I still struggle today—bipolar disorder is, after all, a lifelong illness—but everything is a lot more manageable thanks to the coping techniques Rachel has taught me. I'd say we are a model for therapeutic relationships with boundaries, structure, reliability, mutual respect, and compassion. I never would have thought I'd find that in Rachel when I first landed on her doorstep ten years ago.

I am an engineer by training, not a writer (in fact, I haven't taken a formal course on writing since I was in high school!), and I would be remiss if I didn't acknowledge the individuals who have made my writing stronger. Thanks to Elizabeth DeNoma for providing developmental edits that helped fill some gaps I was missing in my first draft and for encouraging me to continue forward with this project. I'd also like to thank Lisa Rose for helping my prose shine. Every author has doubts about her work, but Lisa helped me believe in this book and took my writing to the next level. I am grateful to the proofreading and newfound friendship of Deirdre Stoelzle, who, by sheer luck, was able to get my book into the hands of Frank Ochberg. I also appreciate the beta readers who took the time to help me fine-tune various sections of my book.

On the topic of publishing, I'd like to thank Nuno Moreira for the sweet cover design, which conveys the chaos of my experience as well as the general themes of isolation and vulnerability. The concept was entirely his based on what he gleaned from the manuscript. I'd say the design is spot on.

Lastly, I would like to acknowledge the Virginia Tech community, who came together following the tragedies mentioned in this book and began the healing process, even if it wasn't enough for me. The friends I made during my time in grad school served a very important purpose of getting me through those dark times, and I wish each and every one of them peace and the ability to let go of the pain. It may come as a surprise that I hold no hard feelings toward Virginia Tech for what transpired. Admittedly, none of us knew what we were doing; nobody thought a mass shooting would ever occur in the quaint little town of Blacksburg at the time. Today—in

2023—mass shootings in America are an entirely different story altogether. My hope is that, by sharing my experience, others will understand the psychological harm caused by mass trauma and more people will be able to get the help and support they need.

About the Author

Ann E. Jeffers, Ph.D., is an Associate Professor of Civil and Environmental Engineering at the University of Michigan in Ann Arbor, MI. She has a Bachelor of Science in Civil Engineering from the University of Pittsburgh, and she has a Master of Science and Doctorate of Philosophy in Civil Engineering from Virginia Tech. Her research focuses on computational methods of analysis, with applications primarily involving structure fires and wildfires. She was co-Editor-in-Chief of *Fire Safety Journal* from 2016-2018, and she has earned a number of awards for her research, teaching, and service over the years. Following her diagnosis with bipolar disorder, Ann became a mental health advocate and a champion for disability rights. She has written a few pieces on mental health for *The Mighty* and *Open Minds Quarterly*. Ann lives in Michigan with her wife and three kids, two of whom were adopted from the foster care system following the events in this book.